Point
v.
Dunstable

Point
v.
Dunstable

Thomas J. Leach
University of the Pacific
McGeorge School of Law

NITA
National Institute for Trial Advocacy

Address inquiries to:

Reprint Permission
National Institute for Trial Advocacy
1685 38th Street, Suite 200
Boulder, CO 80301-2735
Phone: (800) 225-6482
Fax: (720) 890-7069
Email: permissions@nita.org

ISBN 978-1-60156-400-9
FBA 1400

Printed in the United States of America

ASPEN
PUBLISHING

Official co-publisher of NITA.
aspenpublishing.com/NITA

Contents

ACKNOWLEDGMENT

The National Institute for Trial Advocacy wishes to thank Adrian Mendoza, a Portland-based photographer, for permission to use his artwork in this case file.

INTRODUCTORY NOTE

This two-witness-per-side case file tries easily in a half-day schedule: either three hours as a bench trial or with an imagined jury, or about four and one-half hours if one empanels a jury and listens to its deliberations.

The following are suggested time durations:

Pretrial matters: eight minutes per side

Presentation of entire case (opening statements, direct of own witnesses and crosses of opponents' witnesses, and closing arguments): eighty minutes per side

All years in these materials are stated in the following form:

YR-0 indicates the actual year in which the case is being tried (i.e., the present year);

YR-1 indicates the next preceding year (please use the actual year);

YR-2 indicates the second preceding year (please use the actual year), etc.

Electronic files for the exhibits are available for download here:

Website: http://bit.ly/1P20Jea
Password: Point1

Statement of the Case

Plaintiff Joséphine Point is a French citizen residing in Nita City, Nita, USA, where she teaches cinematography at Nita University. She also works independently as a filmmaker, specializing in short features that she describes as "modern interpretations/adaptations/variations of cinema classics."

In YR-4, Point engaged defendant Stanley Dunstable to advise her on the terms of a distributorship agreement with MajorFilms, Inc. Dunstable is an attorney licensed and practicing in Nita, California, and New York, specializing in intellectual property matters. Under the proposed agreement, MajorFilms would undertake to place Point's films in film festivals, specialty ("art") movie houses, and public television programming. The agreement gave MajorFilms certain "alteration rights" to enable MajorFilms to modify the films to suit a targeted audience or market, while also providing assurances to Point that the "essential artistic aspects" of the films would remain unchanged. After negotiations and amendments to the form of agreement, Point and Major Films executed the agreement.

In the fall of YR-4, Point chose the short feature she had created as her Master of Fine Arts thesis, entitled *What Red Balloon?*, for MajorFilms to submit to the Sundance Film Festival as an entrant in the YR-3 event. However, Point learned from one of the preliminary-round judges at the Festival that MajorFilms had altered the print in a way she believed significant: instead of showing a balloon that was light in color, but essentially colorless—because Point's original film was shot in black-and-white—MajorFilms had "colorized" the balloon to make it appear light pink, while the rest of the film remained black-and-white.

Point complained to MajorFilms that the altered print of her film constituted a violation of the terms of the agreement and of her artistic rights in that the appearance of the balloon as essentially colorless (in her original) was a central feature of the artistic statement she was making in the film. MajorFilms replied that it considered the alteration entirely consistent with MajorFilms's alteration rights under the agreement and refused to change the print.

The film won no award or mention at the Festival.

In October YR-3, Dunstable filed suit on Point's behalf against MajorFilms alleging breach of the distributorship agreement. Under the terms of the agreement, the suit was referred to binding arbitration before the Nita Arbitration Forum. Three arbitrators—all drawn from the film industry or related fields—were empanelled by agreement of the parties.

Point contends that in their preparations of the case for the arbitration, and repeatedly throughout the arbitration proceedings, she asked Dunstable to assert, in addition to a breach-of-contract claim, a claim under the European legal concept of *droit moral*, which has been "summarized as including the right of the artist to have his work attributed to him in the form in which he created it." (*See* applicable law: Jury Instructions and Appendix B.) Dunstable did not add such a cause of action on the grounds, inter alia, that in his judgment the claim would weaken, not strengthen, Point's breach-of-contract claim.

The matter went to arbitration hearings in November YR-3. On February 29, YR-2, the panel found in favor of MajorFilms and assessed hearing costs of $27,000 against Point.

Point has now brought this suit against Dunstable alleging legal malpractice in the pursuit of her claim, primarily on the ground of his omission of the *droit moral* issue, but also on grounds of other actions or failures to act.

Witness List

Witnesses for the Plaintiff

Joséphine (Josef) Point

Prof. Frederic (Frederica) Sullivan

Witnesses for the Defendant

Stanley (Estelle) Dunstable

Dr. Ruth (Rufus) Schwenck

All four witnesses may be played as either male or female.

Stipulations/Procedures

1. The case will be tried on liability only.

2. All law relevant to the substantive claims in this case is contained in the Jury Instructions and the Legal Addendum that are part of the case file. Where actual cases are included (*Gilliam*, *Turner*) and actual statutes are referenced (New York Arts and Cultural Affairs Law, Visual Artists Rights Act), the dates and facts have been changed in some instances to coordinate better with the facts of the case file. Participants should rely only on the excerpted versions, as altered, contained in the Legal Addendum.

   Point v. Dunstable is intended to test *only* the participants' trial skills and ethical and professionalism standards, *not* their knowledge of substantive intellectual property (IP) law. Thus, the principles and laws of copyright, Lanham Act, "right of publicity," and all other similar areas of IP law have been excluded from the materials, and no research should be performed or offered in those areas, *except, however,* that the doctrine of *droit moral*, as explicated by the excerpted decisions in *Gilliam v. ABC* and *Turner Entertainment Co. v. Huston* (*see* Legal Addendum) and by the descriptions and discussions in the witnesses' depositions and the experts' reports, *is* to be employed in the litigation of the defendant's alleged malpractice.

3. The Nita Rules of Evidence and Civil Procedure apply to the trial of this case. They are identical to the Federal Rules of Evidence and Civil Procedure.

4. The Model Rules of Professional Conduct are in effect in the State of Nita and may be cited as NRPC (Nita Rules of Professional Conduct).

5. Each witness's complete recollection of the facts of the case is contained in his deposition testimony as provided in this case file. In other words, counsel should assume that with regard to every topic and event covered in the deposition testimony, the witness was asked and responded, and there was no other information available from the witness as to the topics and events covered in the deposition.

6. The parties have stipulated that the exhibits contained within this case file are authentic and, to the extent necessary, original documents within the meaning of Article 10 of the Federal Rules of Evidence. The admissibility of any document or testimony, however, will be determined by the trial judge.

7. The plaintiff must call Joséphine Point and Frederic Sullivan as witnesses in the case. The defendant must call Stanley Dunstable and Ruth Schwenck as witnesses in the case.

8. Both expert witnesses are qualified under Nita Rules of Evidence 702 to testify on all issues discussed in their reports. Notwithstanding this stipulation, an opposing party may cross-examine the expert on the expert's qualifications and may, as a strategy, request that the court exclude the expert's testimony on the ground of insufficient qualifications. However, the court is required to

deny such request. As to the experts' compliance with the requirements of Nita Rules of Civil Procedure 26(a)(2)(B)(iv) through (v)—writings authored and cases testified in as experts—it is stipulated that the information supplied in their reports meets the Rule's requirements; no issue may be raised on that ground.

9. The witness roles are gender neutral. The judges will be instructed to ignore genders, and no argument or cross-examination may attempt to exploit any issue of gender.

10. No witness shall employ a foreign accent in his or her portrayal of the role; specifically as to Josèphine Point, it must be assumed that Ms. Point has been in the U.S. long enough, and is linguistically gifted enough, that she has no trace of French accent remaining.

11. Other than what is supplied in the problem, there is nothing exceptional or unusual about the background information of any of the witnesses that would bolster or detract from their credibility.

12. As to the "relevant legal community" in which the defendant practices, it is stipulated that the Greater Nita City region is a large urban community of about 1.5 million residents, with a civil litigation bar numbering in the several hundreds. Nita is not within the jurisdictional limits of the U.S. Court of Appeals for the Second Circuit.

13. The Statement of the Case is supplied for background information/understanding only and may not be cited in opening statement, examination of witnesses, or closing argument.

IN THE SUPERIOR COURT

FOR THE COUNTY OF DARROW

NITA

JOSÉPHINE POINT, Plaintiff	:	CIVIL ACTION YR-2-1427
	:	
	:	
	:	
STANLEY DUNSTABLE, Defendant	:	JURY TRIAL DEMANDED

PLAINTIFF'S COMPLAINT

Plaintiff Joséphine Point, by and through her undersigned attorneys, hereby avers:

1. Plaintiff, a French citizen residing in Nita City, Nita, is an independent filmmaker specializing in original short features.
2. Defendant Dunstable, a U.S. citizen residing in Nita City, Nita, is an attorney holding himself out as qualified to provide legal services in Nita and elsewhere.
3. Defendant undertook legal representation on Plaintiff's behalf beginning in March YR-4 and continuing through November YR-3 in connection with Plaintiff's business dealings and litigation with MajorFilms, Inc., a New York company in the business of film distribution.
4. In his representation of Plaintiff, Defendant held himself out as qualified to advise Plaintiff on contractual provisions with MajorFilms and to conduct litigation ("the Arbitration") on Plaintiff's behalf to redress a breach of contract by MajorFilms.
5. In his conduct of advising and representing Plaintiff as set forth in paragraph 4 hereof, Defendant failed to abide by the minimum standards of legal competence expected of attorneys practicing in Nita, in the following respects:
   a. Dunstable failed to abide by Point's express desire to make a primary goal of the Arbitration the advancement of the doctrine of *droit moral* as a legal theory for protecting artists' rights generally, and her rights specifically, from alteration, degradation, or mutilation of their artistic works;
   b. Dunstable failed to use the doctrine of *droit moral* as a ground for relief in the Arbitration, which failure Plaintiff avers, on reasonable belief, caused her to lose the Arbitration;
   c. Dunstable failed to investigate adequately the background of the proposed arbitrators and of MajorFilms's expert witness and, as a consequence, failed to discover conflicts of interest and biases that Plaintiff avers, on reasonable belief, affected the outcome of the arbitration;
   d. Dunstable failed to communicate adequately and timely with Plaintiff concerning, inter alia, the arbitrators' backgrounds; the previous and likely continuing close affiliation of Arbitration Chairperson Primus and MajorFilms's expert witness; Dunstable's decision and

reasons for not advancing the doctrine of *droit moral* in derogation of Plaintiff's express goal for the Arbitration; the risk that Plaintiff would be required to pay the Arbitration fees and expenses, which in fact were imposed on her in the amount of Twenty-Seven Thousand Dollars ($27,000); and the true nature of his handling of a previous similar case; and

e. Such other failures and derogations as Plaintiff shall prove at trial.

6. Dunstable's failure to abide by the minimum standard of care, as pleaded in paragraph 5 hereof, was a substantial factor in causing Plaintiff to obtain a worse result in the Arbitration than she would have if Dunstable had not so failed.

7. As a result of Dunstable's negligence, as pleaded herein, Plaintiff has suffered damage to her professional and artistic reputation and such other damage as she shall prove at trial.

WHEREFORE, Plaintiff demands a judgment against Defendant awarding her monetary damages in an amount to be proved at trial plus interest and costs, together with such other relief as is available to her at law or in equity.

Samuel Willis

Samuel Willis, Attorney for
Plaintiff Joséphine Point

Dated and Filed: March 24, YR-2

IN THE SUPERIOR COURT

FOR THE COUNTY OF DARROW

NITA

JOSÉPHINE POINT, Plaintiff	:	CIVIL ACTION YR-2-1427
	:	
v.	:	
	:	
STANLEY DUNSTABLE, Defendant	:	JURY TRIAL DEMANDED

DEFENDANT'S ANSWER AND COUNTERCLAIM

ANSWER

Defendant Stanley Dunstable, by and through his undersigned attorneys, hereby answers the Complaint:

1–4. Admitted.

5–7. Denied.

WHEREFORE, Defendant demands a judgment denying Plaintiff's claim for relief.

COUNTERCLAIM

8. Plaintiff contracted in her Representation Agreement with Defendant to pay all legal fees and expenses incurred in Defendant's representation of her interests.
9. By invoice dated March 5, YR-2 (Exhibit A hereto), Defendant duly billed Plaintiff the amount of fees and expenses incurred in his representation of her interests, in the amount of $17,584.25, which invoice remains owed and unpaid as of the date hereof.

WHEREFORE, Defendant demands a judgment against Plaintiff in the amount of $17,584.25 plus interest and costs.

Angelina Corcoran

Angelina Corcoran, Attorney for
Defendant Stanley Dunstable

Dated and Filed: April 18, YR-2

Exhibit A (*see* Exhibit 15 of this case file)

IN THE SUPERIOR COURT

FOR THE COUNTY OF DARROW

NITA

JOSÉPHINE POINT, Plaintiff	:	CIVIL ACTION YR-2-1427
	:	
	:	
	:	
STANLEY DUNSTABLE, Defendant	:	JURY TRIAL DEMANDED

PLAINTIFF'S REPLY TO DEFENDANT'S COUNTERCLAIM

Plaintiff Joséphine Point, by and through her undersigned attorneys, hereby replies to Defendant's Counterclaim:

8. Admitted.

9. Denied as stated. Admitted that Defendant billed Plaintiff as stated, and that Plaintiff has not paid Defendant's invoice. Denied that the invoice is owed due to Defendant's failure properly to represent Plaintiff, as set forth in Plaintiff's Complaint.

WHEREFORE, Plaintiff demands a judgment denying Defendant's prayer for relief on the Counterclaim.

Samuel Willis

Samuel Willis, Attorney for
Plaintiff Joséphine Point

Dated and Filed: May 13, YR-2

Deposition of Joséphine Point[1]

My name is Joséphine Point. Because my name is French and not so easy for Americans to pronounce (in French, "Pwăhn"), I have simplified it and pronounce it like the English word "point."

My occupation is that of Associate Professor of Fine Arts at Nita University here in Nita City, Nita, where I have been on the faculty since YR-6. I teach Basic and Advanced Cinematography and the History of Cinema, and I oversee the thesis work of candidates for the MFA (Master of Fine Arts) degree.

I was born in France in May YR-36, in a medium-sized city called Pleurisy-sur-Seine, about twenty miles northwest of Paris. By the time I was in high school, Pleurisy had become pretty much a suburb of Paris. At a young age, I was taken often to the movies by my parents, who took a lively interest in all the arts. One of my earliest memories was going to see *Gone With the Wind*, starring Clark Gable and Vivien Leigh—I remember it particularly because I got a big crush on Gable and was heartbroken when my father told me he was no longer alive![2] I also saw all of the English, French, and Italian classics: Truffaut's *The 400 Blows*, Fellini's *La Dolce Vita*, Lester's *A Hard Day's Night*. By the time I was ten years old, I knew I wanted to make a career in some field of the cinematic arts.

After high school in the French system, one specializes immediately in the field one is planning to enter; I attended the Université des Arts Cinématographiques in Paris, where I received my BA in Cinematography in YR-14. I continued there to get my Master of Fine Arts degree in YR-12. My special field of concentration was in short features and particularly in shorts that I described in my master's thesis précis as "modern interpretations/adaptations/variations of cinema classics," as a way of commenting both on the development of film esthetic and technique between the time of the original and that of the remake and on the changes in societal attitudes from the earlier era to the later. My master's thesis film was entitled *What Red Balloon?* I will describe it in more detail when we come to the discussion of the lawsuit that led to this claim I am making against Dunstable.

In YR-11, I moved to New York City to pursue my goal of making a continuing series of short features, but I found that funding was very hard to find and so it became impossible to support myself solely as a filmmaker. Through filmmaking circles I met several of the faculty from the College of Fine Arts at Nita University (NU). They took an interest in my work and suggested that I come to fill a recently vacated position at NU to teach the courses in Cinematography and History of Cinema. I interviewed for the position and also submitted my portfolio of work (the three short films I had completed at that time, including *What Red Balloon?*). They offered me the post, and I began teaching there in

1. If played by a male witness, Josef Point.
2. Or substitute a crush on Vivien Leigh, or on both.

the Fall of YR-8 as an Assistant Professor. I was promoted to Associate Professor in YR-4, which is the rank I currently hold.

In mid-YR-7, when I felt I had my feet well under me in the teaching world, I turned my attention back to my other artistic pursuit—to continue to make my series of short features that I hoped would make a name for me in American and French cinema circles. What many moviegoers may not realize is that there is a lively and very active group of filmmakers who prefer to work in short subjects as opposed to the normal two-hour-long "main feature." It used to be, of course, that at a showing of a regular movie at a Loews or RKO movie theater, first there would come a series of "opening acts," you might say. When I was young, it usually started with Movietone News—short film clips of the news of the preceding weeks—then a cartoon or two—I remember Mickey Mouse, Bugs Bunny, Elmer Fudd, Woody Woodpecker, Wile E. Coyote, and so many others—then a "short feature." Even though these introductory showings have now been replaced in U.S. movie theaters with advertisements and entertainment "news," there remains a flourishing segment of filmmakers who make "shorts." They are shown typically at special festivals for short features, and the Oscars still have an award for Best Short Film.

The reason that "shorts" have not died out, even though no longer shown at regular movie showings, is that they are highly respected by cinema aficionados as a showcase for the cinematographer's talent. That talent, they believe, can be shown to best effect when it is executed on a small "palette," without the need for elaborate costumes, sets, vast troops of extras, and multimillion-dollar budgets. In this respect, short-feature filmmakers are looked on as a sort of "elite" in the world of cinema. My colleague at NU, Giles Goadboy, who is the current Dean of the Fine Arts College, but also has a background in both cinema and stage history, has put it this way: "The makers of big films are comparable to Homer writing *The Iliad* and *The Odyssey*. If they succeed, they have a heroic masterpiece, but if they fail, it's a big mess. Short-feature directors are like haiku masters, who create poetic masterpieces in seventeen syllables." So I felt it would advance my career both as a teacher of cinema arts and as a cinematographer if I continued to specialize in my chosen area of shorts.

From YR-7 to YR-5, I added three more short features to my body of work, bringing my total to six, and I felt this was a sufficient number to enable me to make a foray into the larger world of short-feature public showings. I hoped to have my work recognized first by my peers and then get placements for the films in festivals around the U.S. and in France (where there continues to be a highly educated, sophisticated segment of moviegoers who value the smaller, more artistic works—France has been "movie-mad" for well over 100 years); then to get placements in the small "art" cinemas that still flourish in large U.S. cities and in both medium- and large-size French cities. As an example, I have brought with me to this deposition today an article (Exhibit 1) about a theater in New York that shows works of independent filmmakers. That's the kind of interest I wanted to attract.

Among the filmmakers I know, it is generally considered important, if not essential, to be represented by a strong and well-respected distributor. Movie festivals get so many "anonymous" (i.e., not famous) entries that one really needs a distributor's name and lobbying to get one's film looked at with any attention and chance of making it past the preliminary screenings. I also hoped that a good distributor with the right connections could place my movies with public television stations around the U.S., which would foster both my reputation and hopefully an increased interest in short features among the U.S. moviegoing public. Placements in art theaters and on public television could also bring a decent dollar return.

Dean Goadboy took an interest in my plans, and he recommended to me that I talk with MajorFilms, which he said had an excellent track record in handling smaller filmmakers' work and getting it placed well. He also showed me an article from *Variety*—a copy of which I also brought with me today (Exhibit 2)—about how distributors were consolidating and the bigger ones were getting more name recognition than the smaller ones. Goadboy told me that MajorFilms was one of the big "players," especially for shorts. He put me in touch with MajorFilms's two partners, George Fell and Mabel Swoop. I met with them in MajorFilms's New York office in February of YR-4. They liked my work (I had sent them prints of all of my six shorts), and they enthusiastically invited me to enter into a five-year distributorship agreement whereby I would retain the copyrights to my work, but they would have distribution rights. They would bear all the expenses of placing my work and advertising any successes I might have. If there were fees generated by the showings, we would share those profits on an escalating scale—more for MajorFilms in the first two years of the agreement, when they would be doing a lot of preliminary work without immediate return, but a larger share to me in the later three years, when they said they expected my work could achieve a measure of recognition that would increase its salability.

Fell and Swoop sent me their standard form of distributorship agreement to review (Exhibit 3). I realized that I should get legal advice about it for two reasons. First, I needed to protect my financial and reputational interests. Second, I had heard a lot during my student days in France, and in the years I spent in New York in the world of struggling cinematographers, about how we needed to protect the appearance, content, and artistic integrity of our work, especially when it got into the hands of distributors, who have profit motives that can lead them to make changes to improve salability or placement potential. My American filmmaker acquaintances were interested to learn from me and other European-trained filmmakers about the artistic/legal concept of *droit moral* (for my American friends, we usually simplified the pronunciation of this term as "DWAH maw-RAHL" or we translated it into English, "artistic moral rights"). I had a course in artists' rights when I was getting my French undergraduate degree, and we spent several weeks reading about and discussing *droit moral.*

Droit moral generally refers to an artistic creator's right to protect her work—especially to prevent her work from being altered without her permission. We are used to these concepts in Europe. My American friends agreed that we needed to fight to get ourselves the same kinds of protection here in the U.S. We also discussed how artists in painting, sculpture, photography, etc., had succeeded in getting statutory protection under a law called the Visual Artists Rights Act, but that films were excluded from that protection, so we needed to fight to find some equivalent protection for our film works.

We specifically discussed and took courage from a New York court decision, the *Gilliam* case, where the creators of the Monty Python TV series won a victory against the ABC network when ABC tried to air a version of the Python shows that was so chopped up and "sanitized" (language cleaned up, etc.) that it misrepresented the creators' artistic work. We understood that that decision appeared to recognize *droit moral* as a basis for providing protection for artists, and especially for filmmakers, even though *droit moral* is not generally thought of as a part of American law.

Because of this background, I knew when I was reviewing the proposed distributorship agreement that I should try to build in some language that would give me a basis to argue for *droit moral* protection if I ever needed it. Dean Goadboy told me he had worked with and had a good opinion of Stanley Dunstable, a lawyer here in Nita City. In March YR-4, I met with Dunstable to discuss whether he would represent me by reviewing the agreement.

I got a very good first impression of Dunstable in our meeting. Although he struck me as a little on the young side, he seemed to have a strong background in cases involving artists' rights and copyright issues, especially if they ended up in litigation. Of course, I did not plan on a litigated dispute with MajorFilms, but all my friends, including Dean Goadboy, told me it was good to have a lawyer who knew not only the transactional side of IP, but also the litigation side. Such lawyers understand better than purely transactional lawyers the kind of provisions you need to have in case you ever have to go to court. It also means you are likely to be able to use the same lawyer, who already knows the matter, for any litigation instead of having to find and pay a new lawyer. So I was pleased when Dunstable told me about his litigation background.

I recall that he described a case he had handled for a woman who wrote and starred in a radio quiz show called "Wait, Wait—I'll Tell You" that was very successful on Nita City Public Radio (NPR station KZBT) until the station started interrupting it with call-in participants who they invited to try to guess the quiz answers. The call-ins were not a part of the show that the show's inventor and star wanted, Dunstable said, and so she sued—successfully, he said—for damages and to enjoin the misuse of the show.

I asked specifically, because it was so important to me to try to establish more artists' protections, whether in that case he had used an argument based on *droit moral.* I told him I wanted the agreement with MajorFilms to give us ammunition for protection based on *droit moral,* both to improve our chances of success in the event of disputes and also to strike a blow for artists' rights and protections that could help artists in future cases. Dunstable told me he had used a *droit moral* argument in the radio case, and he believed it was one of the reasons for his successful result there.

Based on all of this, I agreed to hire Dunstable to represent me in my negotiations with MajorFilms. Exhibit 4 is a copy of the representation agreement. Dunstable told me that he advised some inserts and changes to MajorFilms's form of agreement, which he would draft and send me. Dunstable also advised that it would hold my legal fees down if I did all the discussion and correspondence with MajorFilms at this stage and that I should involve him only if some serious legal issue came up.

A few weeks after our meeting, Dunstable sent me some inserts to propose to MajorFilms. I discussed these in a phone call with Mabel Swoop, MajorFilms's president and my main contact there, and she said that after she had looked at it in hard copy she would get back to me on the issue if they had any problem with the new language. So I sent the re-drafted agreement to MajorFilms (Exhibit 5) with a cover letter explaining what our intentions were for the changes (Exhibit 6). I copied Dunstable on the letter and enclosure.

MajorFilms accepted our form of the agreement, with two clarifications. They sent it back to me (Exhibit 7) with a cover letter (Exhibit 8). I called Dunstable and read him the changes MajorFilms had made to paragraph 7. Dunstable told me they were OK. I do not recall whether I read him MajorFilms's cover letter or not—my notes of our telephone call (Exhibit 9) refer to the letter, but I have no independent recollection of discussing the letter specifically. I also do not recall if Dunstable asked me whether there was a letter or anything about the letter. Anyhow, based on his advice, I initialed the changes, signed the agreement, and returned it to MajorFilms. They sent me back a fully signed copy of Exhibit 7.

All of these negotiations took about six months, so our agreement became effective in early Fall of YR-4. MajorFilms immediately asked which of my films I considered ready so that they could submit it for entry at the YR-3 Sundance Film Festival. This was very exciting to me, as this Festival—begun, as most people know, by Robert Redford and attended by Hollywood's elite producers and distributors—is generally recognized by short filmmakers as the best place to get your work known, honored, and then maybe picked up by the art theaters and public television stations. The advertising clout of a listing as a "Sundance Festival Winner" is priceless! Plus, there was an article in the *New York Times* that said that Sundance was increasingly concentrating its interest on the work of independent filmmakers ("indies") (Exhibit 10).

I decided to have MajorFilms submit my first film, *What Red Balloon?*, for two reasons. First, it is kind of a sentimental favorite of mine *because* it was my first. Second, I had had the longest time to work on it—to edit it, bring it up to date with my current filmmaking goals and aesthetics, and make sure it was in the best, most presentable form of any of my works. MajorFilms said they liked my choice and would submit it for the Festival.

The way the Festival works is that all submitted films go through a first evaluation phase to determine which will be final entrants in the Festival. Not every submitted film is accepted, of course. There are too many candidates, and the "first cut" is their way of keeping the number of entrants low (for prestige) and the quality high. Then, the Festival has a nice sort of friendly touch they add: all the filmmakers whose works are accepted as final "entrants" to the competition get not only a confirming letter, but also a telephone call from one of the judges to give the news in person, with a kind of "pat on the back." It's one of the things that makes the Festival so popular with the artists, because it has more of a human touch. So I was very excited when two things happened on the same day in mid-November YR-4: I got a letter saying my film was accepted, and then the phone rang with a call from Randy Lopan, one of the judges of short features.

Randy introduced himself and then told me how pleased he and the other short-feature judge, Noel Newman, had been with my work and how they were looking forward to a very exciting final round of the competition for the eight accepted entrants for short features. In my excitement, I almost missed the next thing he said, but it came as such a surprise to me I asked him to repeat it. He said: "We did wonder about one thing—the title makes it seem like the balloon in your film is meant to be colorless, but the balloon in the print we reviewed was pink, and it stood out from rest of the film that's black and white. Kind of like in *The Wizard of Oz* when Dorothy landed in Oz and it changed from the black-and-white scenes in Kansas to color—except here, we sort of expected it to stay black and white."

I was stunned! The whole point of my film was to make a statement about how the world and aesthetics have changed from the mid-1950s, when the short film *The Red Balloon* was made. My "re-make"—really a variation on the theme of that old classic—was intended to express in film—visually—how colorless the world has become. Every corner you turn in Paris now has a Starbucks or a KFC instead of a French-style café. French kids don't go to visit Versailles on their school field trips—they go to Euro Disneyland. French fashions look to me like all the others: Prada, Dolce & Gabbana, Tommy Hilfiger, or Dior—they're all now just "stores in the mall." My film was meant to show this. The balloon, which every film buff will recognize from the '50s film, is now shown as colorless, like modern society, modern food, modern fashions, modern tourist attractions. So to change the balloon in my film from colorless to colored was an artistic disaster! It totally changed the point of my work.

At that time, I didn't say anything to Lopan about the colorization issue, because I wanted to see if I could fix the problem without jeopardizing my chances in the Festival.

I called MajorFilms right away and got both Fell and Swoop on the line because I wanted them both to hear my complaint and tell me how they were going to fix it. Imagine my amazement when they said they considered that their decision to partially "colorize" the print (only the balloon was shown with any hue—the rest stayed black and white) was a "minor alteration" intended to make the film more attractive to the viewing public, which they said these days doesn't "relate well to black-and-white, because they are so used to bright colors and fast-moving images on the Internet and in video games." I asked them why they hadn't consulted with me before making the change, since clause (b) of the "alterations" section of the agreement gave me that right, along with the right to have a disagreement on the point submitted to a neutral body. They said they considered the change to arise under clause (a), relating to "minor alterations," not to (b) "other alterations." I asked them to change their minds and restore the film to its original condition. They flatly refused on the grounds that they were within their rights under the agreement and also that since it had been accepted by the Festival, it was too late to change it and "upset the apple cart."

There didn't seem to be anything further I could do in time before the films came up for the final judging in mid-December. My film did not win a prize or even Honorable Mention when the results were announced in late January YR-3.

I called Dunstable and told him about the entire incident. We met to discuss it. I asked him if he advised bringing suit against MajorFilms. He said he wanted a few days to think that over and also to determine whether his schedule would allow him to pursue the claim soon enough. Within a few days, he called me back, and we agreed that we would pursue legal action under the terms of the original representation agreement I had with him.

Dunstable was pretty tied up with out-of-town litigation during the spring and summer of YR-3, so it was not until late August that we started to work in earnest on my claim against MajorFilms. Dunstable had pointed out that the agreement with MajorFilms required any claims to be brought in arbitration, not in court, which didn't surprise or worry me since I understood the arbitrators would likely be chosen from the artistic community (artists, artists' representatives, or academics teaching in the arts) or from lawyers practicing in related fields, so their knowledge should help them understand my point of view. Dunstable told me that we would be able to get a lot of information about the proposed arbitrators so that we could get the most favorable panel possible.

Dunstable sent me a draft of the arbitration demand (Exhibit 11A) on September 5, YR-3. I called him back immediately to complain that it made a claim only for breach of the "alterations" provision of the agreement with no reference to a supporting claim based on *droit moral*. He said he would think that over and call me back in a day or two. I called him repeatedly over the next three to four weeks, leaving messages for him to call me—urgently, I began to say as the time dragged on. He did not return my calls. I finally reached him when I called on September 27. I asked when he was going to revise the demand and file it. He said, "Sorry, I got swamped with an appeal from my case from the summer. I'll get on that and get it filed right away." The next week, I got a copy of the demand as he filed it with the Nita Arbitration Forum (Exhibit 11B), and I was amazed to see that he hadn't changed a thing from the first draft—nothing about *droit moral*! When I called to ask about this, he first sounded a bit confused, like he didn't remember what I was talking about, but then he said: "Oh, yeah, yeah, that *droit moral* thing. I decided that it would look odd in an American-style arbitration demand, where they are not used to seeing that kind of claim, so it will work better for us if we just bring it up at the hearings."

Each time we met to prepare my testimony and review the documents we were going to present, I continued to ask Dunstable about pressing the *droit moral* claim. Each time he promised that we would work it in at the hearings. I think he called it an "amended claim to confirm the evidence presented." But when we practiced my testimony (which we did in four separate preparation meetings in October and early November), each time I tried to make references to *droit moral*, he told me not to concern myself in my testimony with the legal framework—"Leave it to me to bring that argument up with the panel," he said.

We had two days of hearings, on November 20 and 21, YR-3. Dunstable never once mentioned *droit moral*, and he did not take any action to amend the demand to include *droit moral* as a basis for relief. I asked him about it at least twice over the course of the two days. His answer was: "It's going fine. I think they are seeing our claim very clearly and very favorably. I'll add it in to my closing argument if I think it will help." But he never did.

On February 29, YR-2, the arbitration panel issued its decision (Exhibit 12), and it was a disaster: a complete denial of relief on my claim and assessment of $27,000 in hearing expenses that I had to pay to the Arbitration Forum, including MajorFilms's part of the fees and expenses! It made me wonder about how well Dunstable had looked into the background of the arbitrators and of MajorFilms's expert witness Edwin Merill. For one thing, it turned out that arbitrator Dupple and our expert, Frederic Sullivan, had had some pretty major disagreements in the past. Was there bad blood, I wondered? We also learned that Dupple (who was a lawyer) had once been a partner in MajorFilms's New York law firm, Oakapple & Murgatroyd, which seemed a little too cozy to me. Second, arbitrator Noble seemed from his dissenting opinion to be really interested in the concept of *droit moral*. Why couldn't we have found this out?

Most importantly, we learned at the beginning of the hearings that arbitration chair Primus had a long previous acquaintance with Merill, but they pretty much pooh-poohed any close relationship that would create a conflict of interest. On the basis of what they told us, Dunstable and I talked about whether we should oppose Primus's continuing to serve. I ended up agreeing with Dunstable's advice that we shouldn't delay the arbitration, especially because I had heard from some of my artist friends that Primus was very pro-*droit moral*, so I thought I was getting a great arbitrator who would fairly listen to my case. But after the hearings I got suspicious and looked around on the web, and it didn't take me long to confirm my fears. A website that reported the work of the Virginia committee Primus and Merill had served on together described Merill as the "mentor" to the committee on the concept, feasibility, and advisability of enacting a *droit moral* statute. It also featured a statement from Primus describing Merill's "leadership" in guiding "newcomers like me [Primus] through this difficult process." Well, if Merill had guided Primus like she said, isn't it likely that Primus listened closely to what Merill said in our arbitration hearings—or really, *didn't* say, since the issue was never raised by us or them—about *droit moral*?

Of course, I didn't know any of this stuff about the arbitrators until afterwards. When we got the proposed names back in late October, Dunstable had me meet with him in his office to discuss them. All he told me was which ones seemed too pro-business and likely to be more favorable to MajorFilms. He didn't discuss their artistic backgrounds at all.

Finally, it is most upsetting to me that Dunstable, despite promising over and over to do so, never asserted my *droit moral* claim. I wanted to strike a blow for artists' rights—

to make a difference for the coming generations of artists—and I feel I made it clear to Dunstable that that was as important to me as any monetary recovery on my claim against MajorFilms. It seems to me he completely ignored my wishes, or at least he never took the trouble to explain why he refused to do what I kept asking him to do. That is why I have filed this suit for malpractice.

I have read the foregoing transcript of my deposition on the date below and find it is a true and accurate representation of my testimony.

Signed: *Joséphine Point* 9/9/YR-2
Joséphine Point Date

STATE OF NITA)
) ss.
COUNTY OF NITA CITY)

Deposition held August 5, YR-2.
Subscribed and sworn before me this 9th day of September, YR-2.

Witnessed: *Harry Gebippe* 9/9/YR-2
Harry Gebippe Date
Certified Court Reporter

DEPOSITION OF STANLEY DUNSTABLE[3]

My name is Stanley Dunstable. I am a licensed attorney in the states of Nita, California, and New York, with a specialized practice in IP (intellectual property) litigation. My firm is a sole proprietorship. I am thirty-nine years old.

I attended Nita University as an undergraduate, graduating in YR-17 with a double major in French literature and comparative studies, which at NU comprised studies in all the arts, with a special emphasis on national (i.e., geographic) artistic characteristics and histories. I received my JD degree from Nita University Law School in YR-14. After a two-year clerkship with the Nita Supreme Court, I returned to Nita City as an associate at the largest—then, and still today—law firm in Nita, Parker & Gould (P&G). Because of my undergraduate training in arts-related matters, and because my law school studies and clerkship had involved me fairly heavily in arts-related cases, my practice concentration was in the IP (Intellectual Property) department. I worked as an associate at P&G until YR-6.

I left P&G with two goals in mind. First, the IP department's and my work covered exclusively the transactional side of this area of law: negotiating and documenting the agreements underlying IP licensing, distributing, copyrighting, and patenting issues. However, in my work I was able to observe the work of subspecialists in IP litigation—the lawyers who take IP cases to court or arbitration when the deals fall through or go south. They seemed to be having more fun than the transactional lawyers, and I felt I had the kind of flair for forensic presentation that this subspecialty requires. But P&G's IP department had made a decision to stay out of the litigation side and to send such cases out to litigation specialists, so I decided to take a chance on setting out on my own. Second, I wanted to have more control over the hours I spent on work. I have many outside interests, including a passion for playing the cello in the Nita City Community Orchestra and the pit orchestra for the Nita City Gilbert & Sullivan Players. I hoped that running my own firm would allow me to pursue both of these goals.

I established my own firm in February YR-6, and the decision proved to be a good one. At that time, no IP litigators in the Nita legal community had as deep a background in the transactional side of IP practice as I did, so I could advertise myself as kind of a "double-barreled shotgun" who knew both sides of the practice (i.e., transactional and litigation). My practice was immediately busy—as the Judge sings in Gilbert & Sullivan's *Trial by Jury*, "The briefs came trooping gaily." Yet as busy as I was right away, I also made the decision not to take on any associates or partners. I suppose you could say I'm sort of a "lone wolf." My staff of one office manager, one secretary, and two paralegals provides me the support I need to manage the cases I handle.

In the first two years of my solo practice—that is, before I took Ms. Point's case (YR-6 through YR-4)—I took on a total of eighteen IP litigation cases. Most of them followed a

3. If played by a female witness, Estelle Dunstable.

pattern that is typical of litigated matters of any kind: initial fact investigation with the client and by search of public records and Internet data; filing of suit (for plaintiff) or answer (for defense); extensive discovery by means of document requests, interrogatories, and depositions; pretrial filings with the court to set the case in trial readiness; and then (if not earlier in the proceedings) settlement of the claim by negotiations based on my and my opponents' assessment of the likely outcome of the trial. From my observation, however, IP litigation is a field in which tempers and egos get pretty stirred up, and the desire for one's "day in court" is perhaps stronger than in other areas of dispute. It seems that the artist's (or the inventor's, or the performer's) pride in what they *created* makes them more interested in "justice" as an end, rather than merely an economic recovery. That varies a lot, of course. But it is one reason why a fairly high percentage of my cases, compared to litigation in other fields, go to trial. Of my caseload in those first two years, twelve of them settled, five were still in litigation when Ms. Point's case came in, and one had been litigated to conclusion. That one does bear on the issues in this case, so I will describe it in greater detail in the context of my discussions with Ms. Point.

When Ms. Point first came to my office on March 15, YR-4, the representation she sought was on the transactional side: she wanted my help in refining the form of a distributorship agreement that MajorFilms, Inc. had proposed to her in her initial discussions with them. This seemed to me a relatively straightforward matter.

Ms. Point explained that she had two goals: first, making a name for herself in the independent filmmaking world by getting her films well placed—and as part of this goal, her eyes lit up a bit when she talked about the possibility of making good money if public television stations picked up her work; and second, establishing better protections for the artistic integrity of filmmakers' work. I got the clear impression that the first was considerably more important to her than the second based on the amount of time she spent discussing each and the higher energy she displayed when talking about the first.

In reviewing the form of agreement that she had from MajorFilms (Ex. 3), I told her it seemed to me well designed to achieve her goal of professional advancement and financial gain—MajorFilms was a great choice for a distributor, and the allocation of percentages was very generous to her as a little-known entrant into this field—but that it was weak on the protections side. I said I would counsel adding some better language and a liquidated damages clause. She decided she wanted to engage me to carry forward this representation, so I gave her my standard representation agreement (Exhibit 4) to review. I urged her to take it away with her and consider it at her leisure, asking me any questions she might have, but she replied that she was a "quick read" and was prepared to enter into the agreement without delay. She signed it, as did I.

We also agreed that unless and until the negotiations got "sticky," it would save her money if she simply sent my re-drafting suggestions on to MajorFilms, without discussion or description (to avoid misunderstandings). If they agreed, that would take care of the transactional issue. If they did not, Ms. Point would re-involve me and we would ratchet it up to the "legal" level.

You ask whether I have notes of this first interview with Ms. Point. I do not. I formed the habit early in my career of keeping case details mainly in my head (other than those that are in the existing case documents—the underlying documentary trail), because it minimizes the risk of long drawn-out and expensive discovery battles over attorney-client privilege and work-product. These days, even the simplest case can require the lawyer to divulge a "'privilege log" that costs his client $5,000 to $10,000 to produce, and that doesn't begin to quantify the damage that can be done to a case if a privilege battle is lost. My first mentor at P&G, Barry Wolf, taught me well: "Use the Bob Ryan Rule (Bob was Barry's mentor): Assume that if you write it down, it will be discoverable. It may not turn out that way, but it will keep you cautious better than any misplaced reliance on privilege or work product."

In our March 15 meeting, Ms. Point mentioned her interest in the European concept of *droit moral* as a source of protection of artists' rights, and she did refer specifically to the rather famous *Gilliam* case from the Second Circuit. I told her about my experience in using that doctrine in the one case I had handled that had gone through trial, successfully for my client. This was the radio game-show case, *Samuels v. KZBT*, which she describes in her deposition. (I did not mention that it was the only case I had tried to completion, as I did not think this would instill in her the confidence she needed.) I told her I thought the argument had been effective. This seemed to be one of the factors that made her decide to retain my services. Consequently, when I turned my attention to the re-drafting of the MajorFilms agreement a week or two after Ms. Point and I first met, I reviewed the *Gilliam* decision to give me ideas about how to incorporate good language for Ms. Point's interests along the lines of *droit moral*.

Towards the end of March I sent her an email suggesting language to include as an alternative paragraph to MajorFilms's paragraph 7:

> Distributor shall have the right at all times to make (a) minor alterations to the Films and (b) such other alterations to the Films as in its opinion are necessary for the successful marketing and placement of the Films. However, no alterations may be made under (b) hereof unless (i) the Artist has agreed to such alterations (which agreement shall not be unreasonably withheld) or (ii) if the Artist does not so agree, the dispute has first been submitted to the Dispute Panel of the Nita Volunteer Lawyers for the Arts (the "VLA Panel"). The VLA Panel's decision shall be final and binding upon Artist and Distributor.

The clause referring disputes to the VLA Panel is one that my colleagues and I at P&G had routinely used in cases similar to this one. I had never seen it invoked, probably because none of the cases I worked on while at P&G had developed into disputes that would have required it. I cannot say definitively whether any of my P&G colleagues' cases had ever seen it invoked, but I never heard them say that they had.

I also wrote for her a simple form of liquidated damages clause (paragraph 8 of Exhibit 7), since it was likely to be difficult to prove measurable, actual damages if MajorFilms breached its obligations under the agreement. And I suggested additional language for paragraph 6 to clarify her rights: "and all other artist's rights except as otherwise provided herein."

In early June, Ms. Point called me to say that MajorFilms had two changes they wanted to make in paragraph 7: (1) to exclude copyright/Lanham Act/right of publicity issues, and (2) to limit the coverage of clause (b) of the "alterations" provisions to "alterations affecting the essential artistic aspects of the Films." She faxed me a copy of the re-drafted form (Exhibit 7—although the form I saw was not yet initialed or executed by Ms. Point). I advised her that the first change was fine—this was never going to be a matter that would turn on copyright/Lanham/publicity principles.[4] But on the second change, I told her she was getting less protection than she had originally aimed for. She said she was comfortable with this, as she was feeling increasing urgency about reaching agreement with MajorFilms in time for them to submit one of her films to the YR-3 Sundance Festival, for which the deadline was approaching. She told me she was seeing a lot of news—and hearing a lot from her friends in the business—about money-making opportunities that could flow from a good result at Sundance. It seemed to me that she was much less interested at this point in the "protect the artists" aspect of the matter, given that she did not mention it in the call and was so ready to accept what I told her was less protective language. Based on this telephone discussion, Ms. Point then executed the agreement with MajorFilms in the revised form they had proposed. She faxed me a copy, without any cover letter or note.

The next contact I had with this matter was when Ms. Point called me in February YR-3 to report her success in getting into the Sundance finals, but her dissatisfaction with MajorFilms's changes to her film, especially since her film did not win an award or an Honorable Mention at the Festival. Given that the Festival had already finished, the only recourse she had against MajorFilms was a suit for damages and to enjoin any later use or showing of the altered print of *What Red Balloon?* We met to discuss the pros and cons of the litigation. It was clear from her account of MajorFilms's response to her complaint to them that there was no quick, "down-and-dirty" way of resolving the matter. The two sides had completely opposing views of the alteration that had been made.

For myself, before I agreed to take the matter to litigation, I wanted to be sure either that the dollar amounts at stake were large enough to justify my taking the case or that there were interesting and novel legal issues that could help me enhance my reputation. Either reason would make the case viable economically. In the first instance, if Ms. Point stood to gain a substantial verdict, the matter would justify my level of fees and expenses. In the second instance, I view this kind of a case as a "loss leader": even if the matter is not substantial enough to warrant my billing the client in full, nevertheless the burnishing that my reputation gets from a high-profile case with newsworthy issues—a case in which I could be seen as helping "make new law"—is better than any advertising I could buy, so I am willing to discount my fees substantially in recognition of these realities.

4. *See* Stipulation 2 of the case file. No issue should be raised concerning the correctness or propriety of this piece of Dunstable's advice to Point. For trial of the case, Dunstable's advice is to be considered correct.

I did not totally exclude some chance of the matter yielding a fairly large return for her. While the lost profits from MajorFilms's failure to market her film appropriately would likely be minimal, still the harm to her reputation and standing in the filmmaking community might be assessed fairly robustly, especially if the arbitrators saw MajorFilms as a "deep pocket," as I expected to portray them. Still, I assessed Ms. Point's case as likely to fall more into the second category, that is, a case with facts and issues that had "sex appeal"—figuratively, not literally, of course, as a twenty-minute short about a balloon drifting in the skies above Paris wouldn't risk even a PG-13 rating. No, the "sex appeal" I refer to was the similarity between her case and the *Gilliam* case involving ABC and the Monty Python fellows. The Python-written musical *Spamalot* had come through Nita City in YR-4 on tour, and it sold out every night, which told me that Monty Python fans are alive and well in this region. That being the case, I foresaw that the local newspapers would pounce on this story about a young Frenchwoman continuing where John Cleese and his cohorts left off: tilting at the corporate windmills of ABC and its counterpart in this case, MajorFilms—an artistic version of *David v. Goliath*. So in addition to the primary goal of litigating Ms. Point's rights, I saw this as a chance for me to make a large stride forward in staking out a claim to being Nita's premier IP litigator. That goal, I will admit, was threatened a bit by the arrival in Nita of Tom Tolloller. Tom had handled the plaintiffs' case in *Gilliam* when he was a partner at the large New York firm of Coxe & Baux, but shortly after I started my own firm, P&G changed its mind (largely, I believe, because of Tom's success in *Gilliam*) about developing an IP litigation arm. In early YR-5, P&G lured Tom from New York to Nita City as a lateral partner, and in gossip over lunch or drinks with friends still at P&G, I gathered that Tom was rapidly becoming a major power in the P&G hierarchy.

Ms. Point explained her artistic goals for *What Red Balloon?* and how she felt those goals had been subverted by MajorFilms's unilateral changes to her film print. I believed she had a decent case based on breach of contract, in that MajorFilms had blown right past her rights under clause (b) of the "alterations" section of the Agreement and appeared to be defending their actions as falling solely under clause (a) concerning "minor" alterations. That seemed to me a stance that would strike the arbitrators as high-handed, enhancing the *David v. Goliath* aspect of the case. For all these reasons, I agreed to carry forward the litigation of Ms. Point's case. I told her that as soon as my heavy case load for the spring and summer eased up (I was scheduled to try two large cases in June and August, and to complete discovery in another large case by mid-September), I would turn my attention to drafting and filing the demand for arbitration on her behalf.

You ask whether the subject of basing Ms. Point's claim partly on *droit moral* came up between me and Ms. Point at this litigation planning meeting. I do not recall that, at least not in those terms. She did bring up the subject again—recall that we had discussed it in the initial, "transactional" phase of this matter—but it seemed to me she was simply "thinking out loud" about her own European background in the legal theories that support artists' claims *there*. I did not understand her to be asking me to put forward a *droit moral* claim for her in a U.S. action based on U.S. law—if I had thought that was her request, I am confident I would have disabused her of any serious thought of pressing such a claim, for reasons I will get to when I discuss the conduct of the actual arbitration. But as I say, this discussion of *droit moral* was very brief, and I said almost nothing on the subject—I listened to her talk about it, then I moved the discussion to more useful topics.

Yes, it's true, as I mentioned earlier in this deposition, that I had used an argument in the *Samuels* radio quiz-show case that could be analogized to one based on *droit moral*, but there is an important distinction here. In *Samuels*, I carefully avoided the use of the foreign term and simply presented it as an overriding equitable concept—fair treatment of artists in protecting the integrity of their work, which is really the only "property" they have of value.

As soon as I was able after my summer cases calmed down, I drafted a proposed demand for arbitration (Exhibit 11A) and sent it to Ms. Point for her review. When I did not hear back from her with any concerns, I had it filed with the Nita Arbitration Forum in early October (Exhibit 11B). No, I do not recall getting any calls from Ms. Point about the draft I sent her. I do recognize Exhibits 13A through 13D as telephone message slips of the kind used in my office, and the initials on them are those of my secretary, Honour More, so I have no doubt they are genuine. But I do not recall any further action on those. Normally, I check the box "SD Returned Call" with a note of the time and date, but sometimes in the press of business I forget to do so, so the fact that these four slips do not bear such markings does not mean I didn't return her calls. It may be that I called back, left her a message saying I was returning her call, and then heard nothing further from her—but I do not have a recollection of that one way or the other.

I do recall that at least once when we were preparing her testimony Ms. Point asked me whether it would be a good idea to add a claim based on *droit moral*. As best as I recall, I told her that the best strategy in arbitrations was to wait until we got a sense of the arbitrators' backgrounds, experience, and, most importantly, attitudes and then to conform our case theory and the supporting testimony to make the best appeal to that particular panel.

In October, we went through the process of choosing the arbitrators. The selection is done in three steps: 1) the Forum sends a list of ten names with brief CVs; 2) each side is entitled to oppose any of the names "for cause" and to eliminate ("strike") two of the remaining names; 3) the Forum then picks three arbitrators from the remaining names and appoints one of them the chairperson.

There were no particular surprises on the list of candidates. According to their CVs, all were experienced lawyers, former judges, or professionals in the arts fields (administrators, agents, academics, etc.), and they all had good backgrounds in IP cases or, at least, cases involving arts-related claims. I had my paralegal, Patience Porter, research them further on the Internet, and she reported back to me that none seemed to have any background that would support a challenge for cause. She did not give me any details beyond my particular interest in assessing whether any of them seemed more defense oriented. Her report to me was oral, not written.

Yes, this was the first time I ever actually went through the arbitrator selection process, but I had heard it described often by litigation counsel to whom we had referred out our clients' cases while I was at P&G, so I felt I understood how it should be done.

In consultation with Ms. Point, we struck two who seemed a bit too corporate friendly. MajorFilms's lawyer, Joe Flume, whom I know well from other cases we have handled, struck two who I am sure he thought were too liberal and plaintiff friendly or artist friendly. "Long-hairs," he calls them. As a result, the Forum appointed Emily Primus, H.D. "Hod" Dupple, and Tertius Noble, with Primus to serve as chair.

The two days of hearings in late November went pretty much as I expected. The narrow battleground between the two sides was over whether the colorization of the balloon in the print that MajorFilms submitted to the Sundance Film Festival was a "minor" alteration under clause (a) of the "alterations" section of the Agreement or one that should have been handled under clause (b), which would have given Ms. Point certain appeal rights before MajorFilms could be allowed to continue with the alteration. We showed the panel three comparative still frames taken from the full movie "prints": one from the original short *The Red Balloon* (Exhibit 14A), one with a colorless balloon (Exhibit 14B, Ms. Point's version), and one with the balloon colorized light pink (Exhibit 14C, MajorFilms's version). We also showed them the "Woody/Tinny" clip from the Monty Python shows that had been an exhibit in the *Gilliam* case, together with an edited version to show what ABC's version had looked like (it was described in footnote 12 in *Gilliam)*, which I argued to them showed by comparison that the change to Ms. Point's film was at least as major a departure from her intent as were the editings that ABC had done to the Python shows.

By the afternoon of the second day of hearings, the arbitrators took over a lot of the questioning, as I understand is typical of arbitrations, where the panel is expected to bring its own knowledge and background to bear on the issues in the case. It appeared to me the arbitrators were leaning toward a view that the case turned in large part on what kinds of changes the parties intended to be considered "minor," and they asked several pointed questions of Ms. Point as to how she responded to MajorFilms's letter (Exhibit 8). To me, the implication of their questions was that MajorFilms had staked out a fairly broad definition of "minor"—broad enough to encompass the colorization change—and that Ms. Point had not countered with any narrower definition that would give the panel a hook on which to hang a pro-plaintiff view of the term.

MajorFilms's case was pretty strong, I thought, judging from the arbitrators' reception of it and their questions. In particular, MajorFilms's president, Mabel Swoop, and its expert witness, Edwin Merill, both testified that the colorization was a "minor" change, but that if it was not, it still did not adversely impact the "essential artistic aspects of the Film" so as to trigger the dispute provision of clause (b). They contended that the light pink color of the balloon could well be read as suggesting that while the world was trending dangerously towards the homogenization that Point was targeting, not all hope was lost. A faded balloon was not yet a colorless one, and if the world would wake up to the danger, total homogenization was avoidable. They explained that this interpretation carried forward the true spirit of Point's film, but in a way that was more accessible to U.S. audiences. I saw at least two of the arbitrators nod their heads noticeably at these points of the testimony (nodding in agreement, that is—not in drowsiness).

Particularly as concerns the *droit moral* issue, it is true that Ms. Point asked me several times during the two days of hearings, and again just before I made my summation argument to the panel, whether an argument based on *droit moral* could be helpful. In each instance, I gave her my considered professional judgment that introducing *droit moral* at this late stage of the proceedings would likely seem like a desperation move and would, accordingly, weaken our breach-of-contract claim. Since the arbitrators appeared to me to be taking a quite legalistic, contract-based approach to the case, I believed that a fancy alternate theory based on a foreign concept and term—heck, even its name is French!—at best could not help our case and at worst could hurt it.

I did, of course, argue the equitable side of the case: how in fairness to artists their work should be protected from alteration that affected their artistic intent. The arbitrators displayed no particular interest in this line of argument, however. Their questions that followed appeared to me to signify they were returning to the contractual provisions as controlling over any equities.

I understand that Ms. Point is raising in this present case a concern about a conflict of interest she seems to feel I did not handle correctly. MajorFilms's expert witness Merill was listed as an "arts administrator" from Virginia. At the outset of the first day of hearings, MajorFilms's attorney, Joe Flume, disclosed to the panel and to us that Merill was acquainted with Chairperson Emily Primus. He said that Primus had been the head of a task force for the Virginia Endowment for the Arts (VEA), charged with studying the feasibility of passing a *droit moral* type of legislation similar to the federal VARA (Visual Artists Rights Act). According to Flume, Merill had also served on the committee with Primus, and they had gotten to know each other fairly well in that working relationship. However, that committee's work ended in YR-8 without any legislation being passed, and Primus and Merill had met only coincidentally at arts events in the intervening years. Primus confirmed this description of the relationship between the two.

I consulted with Point as to whether, in light of this arguable conflict of interest, she wanted to postpone the arbitration for the appointment of a new chairperson. She said no, that she was eager to get on with it, especially because the talk she had heard about Primus was that Primus was "pro *droit moral*," so she thought getting such a great arbitration chair answered any concern we might have about undue influence from Merill.

Later, Point did report to me that after the hearings she had found a website from back in YR-7 reporting on the VEA committee's work, which Point said made Merill sound a lot closer to Primus that had been described to us. However, since we had seen no sign during the hearings that Primus gave more attention or credence to Merill than to the other witnesses, I do not see this as a defect in the proceedings. Indeed, since Merill addressed the issues only as contract issues, consistent with MajorFilms's approach to the case, and did not mention *droit moral* at all, I cannot see how his relationship with Primus could have had any improper influence on the outcome.

The arbitration decision (Exhibit 12) was certainly not what Ms. Point or I hoped for, but, quite frankly, that is par for the course in arbitration (and, for that matter, in jury and bench trials). We lawyers consider trial a crapshoot, and those of us who do arbitrations say "arbitration is just a better-informed crapshoot" (because we have more knowledge about the decision makers' backgrounds and, via their questions at the hearings, about the view they are taking of the case). I do not read dissenting arbitrator Noble's reference to *droit moral* as suggesting that we would have gotten a better result by incorporating a *droit moral* argument into our claim. I just think he was showing off by proving that he could speak two words of French.

It is unfortunate that in addition to losing on her claim, Ms. Point was assessed the hearing costs, but that was a risk she faced from the beginning, as was spelled out in our representation agreement (Exhibit 4). The costs are in line with other arbitrations, as I understand it: filing costs are $2,000, plus hearing costs of $250 per day per party, plus arbitrators' compensation at $200 per hour. For an arbitration like this one, the arbitrators likely spent two preparation days, two hearing days, and one decision day at eight hours per day.

My fees, based on my billing rate of $400 per hour, totaled $16,800. Expenses were $784.25. No, I did not consider discounting my fees, because the case did not turn out to have the kind of publicity appeal that would have warranted such action. My final bill (Exhibit 15) is still outstanding, which gives rise to my counterclaim against plaintiff asking for an award directing her to pay what she owes. The hours expended were those needed to meet with her and discuss the matter, to advise her on the distributorship agreement, to consult on the advisability of and the strategy for the arbitration against MajorFilms, and to conduct the arbitration. It is true that the bill does not reflect time expended on research (except for the hours of my paralegal, Patience Porter, investigating the proposed arbitrators' backgrounds), because I considered that I knew well enough how such a case should be framed and litigated. I did not need to add to Ms. Point's legal fees by conducting research in this field of law that is my specialty.

The reason the fees and expenses from my YR-4 representation of Point in the negotiation of the distributorship agreement were not billed until after the arbitration was complete is that Ms. Point requested this. She said that her finances made it difficult for her to pay the YR-4 charges until after she had begun to realize some returns on her agreement with MajorFilms. She was hopeful that the relationship would add to her income fairly early on. Then, after the disagreement arose with MajorFilms, she hoped to pay my charges through her recovery in the arbitration. Given her limited resources, I was willing to bear the delay in payment. However, in no way was this a contingent fee agreement, as our representation agreement makes clear.

I have read the foregoing transcript of my deposition on the date below and find it is a true and accurate representation of my testimony.

Signed: Stanley Dunstable 11/11/YR-2
Stanley Dunstable Date

STATE OF NITA)
) ss.
COUNTY OF NITA CITY)

Deposition held October 9, YR-2.
Subscribed and sworn before me this 11th day of November, YR-2.

Witnessed: Harry Gebippe 11/11/YR-2
Harry Gebippe Date
Certified Court Reporter

REPORT OF PROF. FREDERIC SULLIVAN[5]

I have been retained by plaintiff Joséphine Point and her counsel as an expert witness in her malpractice case against attorney Stanley Dunstable. I served also as her expert witness in the arbitration against MajorFilms. I submit this report to summarize my opinions and the bases for them.

I am a Professor of Fine Arts at the Fairfax College of the Arts located in Philadelphia, where I have taught since YR-37. I did my undergraduate work (BA, YR-43) and my MFA (Master of Fine Arts YR-41) at American University in Washington, DC. After that, my career path coincidentally resembled Ms. Point's, as I spent about five years in New York City working as an independent filmmaker specializing in short features. I had some success there. My two best-known works were *15 Minutes with Andy*, a film that consisted entirely of watching Andy Warhol sleep for fifteen minutes, and *The Happy Journey from Ithaca to Meriden @ 8 MPH*, a documentary about a drug-running ring and its confrontations with the New York State Police.

I began teaching at Fairfax as an adjunct instructor in cinematography in YR-37, joined the faculty full time in YR-35 as an assistant professor, then was promoted to associate professor in YR-32 and to full professor in YR-30. My main interest has always been short films. I write film reviews frequently for the *Villager* and *Village Voice* newspapers. I have published two books: *Short but Sweet: A Guide to the Best in Short Features* (Koko Press, YR-6), a listing of the top short features from 1950 to the present, and *How to Market Your Short Film* (Dauntless Publishing, YR-4), a how-to manual for budding short-feature filmmakers.

A secondary, but still very important, interest of mine is the campaign of filmmakers to obtain the best legal protection they can for the artistic integrity of their work. I became a member in YR-32 of a committee of the New York chapter of Volunteer Lawyers (NYVLA) for the Arts, the goal of which was to lobby with lawyers and legislators to encourage the adoption of statutes or decisions relying on the European concept of *droit moral*. First, I took four weekend training sessions with NYVLA on the theory and practice of *droit moral*. I then began giving talks and participating in panel discussions around the country, organized by local VLA chapters, to spread the word. In part as a result of our work, New York passed a *droit moral* type of artists' protection statute, New York Arts and Cultural Affairs Law § 14.51 to 14.59, in YR-26. We worked as consultants to support the plaintiffs' research and case presentation in *Gilliam v. ABC*, and were, of course, gratified when in YR-21 that decision gave a resounding victory to the idea that *droit moral* can be used as a ground for recovery in U.S. courts. The committee has since that time continued its work to emphasize the importance of such statutes, and our efforts have gained new attention since the passage of the federal Visual Artists Rights Act (VARA) in YR-18.

5. If played by a female witness, Frederica Sullivan.

Because of my increased and continuing interest in the legal side of these matters, I decided that a law degree could be useful to me, so I attended the four-year night program at Calverly University in Philadelphia, where I received my JD in YR-21. I am admitted to the Pennsylvania bar, though I have never practiced. I am not admitted to practice in Nita. I have provided legal advice gratis to artist friends periodically over the years as a kind of pro bono service.

I have testified as an expert witness on two occasions. The first time was in hearings before the Pennsylvania Legislature's Committee on Intellectual Property Legislation. The hearings concerned the question of passing an artist's-rights protection statue similar to New York's; no action was taken as a result. The second time was as an expert for an artist complaining of misuse of his work, and in that respect the case resembled Ms. Point's case against MajorFilms. I was recognized by the court in that case as qualified to give my expert legal opinion. I did refer to *droit moral* in my testimony, and it was not excluded by any objections or court rulings, but I cannot say (because I do not remember it being clear from the outcome of the case) whether the concept played a part in the decision.

I have never before testified as an expert on legal malpractice. However, my law studies covered ethics and professional responsibility, and as a result of contacts I made in my VLA activities, I have been serving since YR-2 as a member of the Philadelphia Bar Association's Professional Guidance Committee, which reviews and issues opinions on ethical issues under Pennsylvania's equivalent of the Nita Rules of Professional Conduct (NRPC). To prepare my opinion in the current matter, I reviewed the law of Nita as it relates to legal malpractice. I also reviewed the pleadings, the depositions of Point and Dunstable, the arbitration decision, and the documents exchanged by the parties, including the exhibits presented in the arbitration.

Since YR-13, I have served every year as a final-round judge for short films at the Sundance Film Festival. YR-13 was the first year that Sundance gave awards for short features, so it was a particular honor to be asked to be an inaugural-year judge. There are two judges who screen the submissions at the preliminary stage, yielding eight films as finalists. There are three finals judges—neither of the preliminary-round judges serves on the final round, so the voting for the winner and the honorable-mention award is entirely separate from the preliminaries. Each finals judge votes confidentially from the other two, by written and sealed ballot, rating the eight finalists in order. Thus, the film with the lowest total number in the voting is the winner, and the second-lowest gets the honorable mention award. If there is a tie for either of the top two slots, the judges vote—again, confidentially—to break the tie. After the voting is finished and the winners decided, the judges do see the tallies, so they know how the eight finalists did. While the competition continues, my fellow judges and I usually talk informally about our views of the finalists and why we voted as we did.

I recall the submissions and the voting in the YR-3 festival very well, especially since I reviewed the matter shortly afterwards in order to testify for Ms. Point in the MajorFilms arbitration held later the same year. Point's film, *What Red Balloon?*, impressed me as beautifully made and a very striking work for such a relative newcomer in filmmaking. The cinematography—the *look* of the film—was both antique and modern in a way that struck me as hard to achieve, so I knew the auteur (that's the standard cinema term for a film's maker—pronounced "oh-TURR"—it means "author" in French) had remarkable talent. But I was puzzled by the film's message, which seemed confused to me.

Of course I recognized that the film referred back to the 1950s short classic, *The Red Balloon*. And I picked up in the first minutes of the film the social comment being made: that the world around us had lost most of its defining differentiation. The little and big details of our surroundings, which in decades past made France noticeably different from America, America different from China, China different from Czech Republic—all were being lost in a sort of "world homogenization." All of this came out of the flat, colorless look of the film.

The confusion I speak of is that when the balloon first appeared and started to float up into the Parisian skies, I expected it to look as washed out as the rest of the scenery. But it was light pink! It was in color! The entire rest of the film was black and white. So I came away from the viewing with a disappointed feeling, that Point had formulated an excellent, clear message, but had lost it partway through the production. In a sense, I felt she had "chickened out" on making the bold statement that she had intended to make. For that reason, I scored it low in my ratings. The other two judges did, too, so it finished way back in the pack of eight finalists. The other judges had their own views of the films, which did not match mine in all respects, and they had somewhat different criticisms of Ms. Point's film, but they did both mention that they thought the color of the balloon muddied the message. I told them that if it hadn't been for the colorization, I had the film ranked solidly for Honorable Mention, at least, and they both seemed to agree with me—they both nodded their heads vigorously, and I recall one of them, Elsie Carruthers, saying, "Yes, Honorable Mention. So did I." An Honorable Mention, as you may know, at a festival with the reputation of Sundance is pretty much a "meal ticket" for a filmmaker like Point who is trying to make a name for herself.

When I was retained as Ms. Point's expert in the arbitration with MajorFilms, I learned that the color had been imposed by MajorFilms, not by Point, and that this was her main contention in the dispute. In my testimony, which came on the first day of the arbitration, November 21, I strongly supported her claim that the change constituted an infringement of her artistic rights, and was certainly *not* a "minor alteration" under the distributorship agreement. Instead, it did direct and measurable damage to what the agreement referred to as "the essential artistic aspects" of the film.

I spoke as vigorously in my testimony as I could, but of course I had to answer the questions that were put to me. I could not simply make a speech from my own vantage point. Point's attorney, Dunstable, was the one who hired me, and I had learned early in my days as an expert witness that one must follow the instructions of retaining counsel. So, because Dunstable did not ask me any questions that pointed me in the direction of commenting on the protections that *droit moral* would give Point, I did not have the chance to advance this argument on her behalf. None of the arbitrators asked me questions that invited reference to *droit moral*. When I finished my testimony, I felt disappointed that we had not been able to take a stand to advance the cause of *droit moral* in U.S. cases.

MajorFilms's expert, Edwin Merill, was called to testify on the second day of the hearings. He made a very smooth, glib appearance, in my opinion, but I felt he was selling the arbitrators a load of garbage, quite frankly. He gave his opinion that the colorized print of the film still conveyed a clear message about the decline of national differences and distinctiveness and therefore that MajorFilms's decision to colorize it for "salability" to U.S. audiences was "plausible." Under *droit moral*, however, what he said was basically meaningless: no self-respecting art expert would ever suggest that anyone other than the artist herself can change the art work for "plausible reasons"! That's like saying the non-artist can, by self-appointment, substitute his artistic concept for the artist's—a ludicrous suggestion that contradicts the expansive protective concept of *droit moral*. Even a small change, like the color of the balloon in Ms. Point's film, can make a complete change in the artistic message. We can find examples throughout the reported cases in which artists' rights were litigated, but we really need look no further than this case to see how that is so. In the Sundance Film Festival, the color of the balloon made the difference between an Honorable Mention and finishing far down the list of finalists.

After the hearings, but before the decision came out in early YR-2, I did some checking into the backgrounds of the arbitrators. For one thing, arbitrator Hod Dupple and I had had some pretty strong disagreements in the past, on various panel appearances. When I heard he was on the panel—about two weeks before I testified—I did not think at that time that those incidents raised concerns about my appearing as an expert. Dunstable did ask me if I knew any of the arbitrators, and I told him of my acquaintance with Dupple. He did not ask me about our disagreements, and, as I have said, I did not think they were disabling, so I did not mention them on my own. I did tell him that Dupple was known as an expert in French shorts from the '50s and '60s, so he certainly knew *The Red Balloon* well and would, I thought, quickly grasp the importance of the balloon being white, not pink, in Point's remake. Dunstable seemed satisfied with that information and did not ask me anything further about Dupple.

Anyway, because Dupple's questions and body language during the hearings told me that he wasn't buying our case very much, my concern about whether I had initially assessed his attitude correctly led me to check up on his more recent background and experience. That's when we found out that he had once worked as a partner in the firm that represents MajorFilms in New York.

I also checked the other two arbitrators. I was surprised to learn that arbitrator Noble seemed to be a strong supporter of the *droit moral* movement. He even had written an article for the New York VLA newsletter entitled "Why Is the U.S. Less *Moral* than France?" In the article, he urged that artists and their representative take a more vigorous stand to fight for the adoption of *droit moral* in U.S. cases. He also suggested language for contract clauses that could give support for a *droit moral* argument. I wondered why Dunstable had not mentioned this—to me, to Point, or in the arbitration proceedings. It did *not* surprise me, therefore, when Noble filed his dissent to the arbitration award stating his view that *droit moral* should have given Point some or all of the relief she was requesting.

Finally, I think it is significant that in the agreement, MajorFilms agreed to have any arbitration held in Nita, not in New York (MajorFilms's home base) and governed by Nita, not New York, law. To me this is an indication that MajorFilms was eager to stay away from the venue where *droit moral* had gained its strongest foothold in the case law—the *Gilliam* case—and where there is a state statute (New York Art and Cultural Affairs Law § 14.51 through 14.59) giving *droit moral* type protections to artists.

For all these reasons, it is my expert opinion that Dunstable failed properly both to carry forward Ms. Point's goals for her case against MajorFilms and to present her case competently and that these failures were a contributing factor to her loss in the arbitration.

I did not charge expert witness fees for my testimony on Ms. Point's behalf in the arbitration, nor am I doing so in this case. Instead, I view my expert witness service as another step in my efforts on behalf of all artists to protect their rights and to be properly and competently represented in the enforcement of those rights. However, my expenses (travel, lodging, meals, etc.) are reimbursed.

Frederic Sullivan

Dated: January 21, YR-1

ADDENDUM: REPONSE TO EXPERT REPORT OF DR. RUTH SCHWENCK

I have read the expert report of Dr. Ruth Schwenck and add this response.

As to compliance with the standard of care expected of attorneys practicing in Nita, I come to very different conclusions than Schwenck.

First, it appears that Dunstable substituted his judgment as to Ms. Point's *goals* for the arbitration in place of hers. As I read the record, she made it very clear that a primary goal was to promote the use of *droit moral* as an available tool for protection of artists' rights, *even if it did not win the arbitration for her, in part or outright.* I have read nothing in the literature or case law concerning NRPC 1.2 to suggest that this is not a proper goal for a client to have and insist upon in litigation she is paying for. And Rule 1.2 assigns the decision on "the purposes to be served by legal representation" to the client, unless the lawyer has limited the scope of the representation, which Dunstable did not do. Moreover, Dunstable and Schwenck overstate the case when they portray Dunstable's approach as concerning only the *means* of the litigation, as if that fully answers the question under Rule 1.2. It does not. Section 21 of the *Restatement of the Law (3d) Governing Lawyers*[6] provides clearer guidance than Rule 1.2; it states in Comment *d—Client Instructions*, that:

- a client may give instructions to her lawyer (and, as I read Comment *d* together with Comment *b*, the *Restatement* draws no distinction here between *goals* and *means*—the client may give instructions as to *both*);

- the lawyer may advise the client of the advantages and disadvantages of a proposed client decision and seek to dissuade her from adhering to it;

- the lawyer may not continue a representation while refusing to follow a client's continuing instruction; and

- the lawyer may, after obtaining court permission, withdraw from the representation if he considers the instruction imprudent or that it renders the representation unreasonably difficult.

While I do not consider that Dunstable's and Point's differing views on using *droit moral* had advanced so far as to require or even recommend Dunstable's withdrawal, from my review of the course of the representation he failed to consult and communicate adequately with Point on this issue, as required by both Rule 1.2 and the *Restatement.*[7]

---

6. *See* Appendix B: Legal Addendum.

7. As compared with a "large, affluent client," an individual layperson client like Point is "far more dependent on [her] lawyer, with little access to information. . . . Thus, the paternalistic lawyer may, if he . . . chooses, exercise nearly full control over the representation, presenting a limited range of choices to the client or sometimes none at all." Burns & Lubet, *Division of Authority between Attorney and Client,* YR-7 U. Ill. L. Rev. 1275, 1279.

As a result, he did not merely substitute his judgment on the goal of the litigation for hers; worse, he did not pay sufficient attention to realize or to remember what this primary goal was and then to discuss the pros and cons of it with her. Every time Point brought it up to him, it seemed to be news to him, as if she were raising it for the first time, whereas according to her recollection as set out in her deposition, she emphasized it every time they met or spoke on the phone. His apparent inattention also ties in with my opinion below concerning his failure to communicate.

From my own experience in New York and from reading the history of the passage of VARA, I can affirm that the repeated use of and reference to *droit moral* in legislative hearings and court cases like *Gilliam v. ABC* accounts for our success in getting the New York artists' rights law and the federal VARA enacted. Ms. Point wanted to use her case against MajorFilms in the same way to promote the adoption or recognition of such a law in Nita, and in my opinion she was entitled under the principles of NRPC 1.2 to have that objective carried forward by her attorney, following her instruction as provided in the *Restatement*.

Second, I find Dunstable's feeble efforts to investigate the backgrounds of the arbitrators and MajorFilms's expert witness shockingly negligent. I can find no other adequate description for it. He virtually admits that the only background he asked his paralegal to check was how "business oriented" the arbitrators were, that he did no research of his own, and that he did not ask Ms. Point or me what we knew about them or what we could find out about them from our contacts in the art world. It is no wonder, then, that he did not uncover a) the suspiciously close connection between Primus and Merill, b) Dupple's former connection with MajorFilms's New York law firm, and c) Noble's favorable view of *droit moral*, which certainly suggests—now, in hindsight—that *droit moral* should have been featured front and center in the arbitration. This last point is confirmed by Noble's dissent to the Arbitration Decision. Dunstable violated NRPC 1.3, pure and simple.

In addition, Dunstable's failure to investigate is probably explained by his inexperience in arbitration practice. He admits in his deposition that he had never before arbitrated a case and had in fact only tried one previous case. Not only that, he appears to me to have spent insufficient time in preparation of the arbitration, in violation of NRPC 1.1.

Third, Dunstable fell down badly on the attorney's duty to communicate regularly and fully with his client, NRPC 1.4. I need say little on this other than to refer to Schwenck's summary of Dunstable's failures in this regard (Schwenck Report, paragraph 3), which to me sets out clearly an itemized list of the communications Dunstable was required to make and did not. I would add only these two points:

- Schwenck dismisses the list as "minor" examples of the kind of complaints disappointed litigants have and opines that Dunstable's efforts to communicate were "reasonable." If each one is taken alone, that might be so. Taken as a pattern of non-communication, they are negligent, especially when combined with his failure to discuss and advise her on her *droit moral* goal (*see* discussion above).

- Dunstable says he never takes notes on his meetings with clients. I find that extraordinary. I always take notes on my meetings with clients, and so does every other lawyer I know. If he claims that he can rely on his memory, this case proves him wrong. He forgot, not simply once, but repeated times, what Ms. Point told him about wanting to emphasize *droit moral.*

Fourth, and most pointedly from the point of view of causation of Ms. Point's loss of the arbitration, in my opinion Dunstable completely botched the strategy of how to win Point's case against MajorFilms. Schwenck's defense of his strategy is equally ill founded.

Not being a filmmaker or particularly trained in *droit moral*, Schwenck has failed to grasp the power of that doctrine to reach beyond contract terms or tort principles, to impose a higher standard of protection for an artist's right to the integrity of her work. This case is an ideal example to illustrate the differences.

According to Schwenck and, apparently, to Dunstable and MajorFilms (since they all reached the same conclusion), *droit moral* and the provisions of paragraph 7 of the agreement are coterminous. Thus, Schwenck says, "*droit moral* does not change the analysis of paragraph 7(a) and (b) of the agreement" under principles of contract interpretation or equity. That is just flat wrong.

Droit moral safeguards an artist's work from *any* change, notwithstanding contract provisions to the contrary. Thus, *droit moral* would have provided a lens through which the arbitrators would have viewed the change in Point's film much more sympathetically, in this sense: Given that *droit moral* provides such vigilant protection of the artist's work, the arbitrators would likely have construed the contract term "essential artistic aspects of the Film" much more expansively.

To put this another way, within the framework of *droit moral*, it would have been virtually impossible for MajorFilms to persuade the panel that the *distributor* could supply *its own rationale* for an *altered* message of the film, replacing the *artist's*. Point said she made the film to show that the world *has* become colorless. MajorFilms said its change conveyed that the world was *becoming* more colorless, but wasn't entirely there yet. Parroting what MajorFilms's expert, Merill, opined at the arbitration, Schwenck and Dunstable say this revised theme is "plausible." Respectfully, and to respond to Schwenck's invitation, plausibility and four dollars will get them a latte to split between them. Under *droit moral*, no one—buyer, distributor, licensee—can change the artist's work. That is why the concept should have been presented and argued to the panel.

I find Schwenck's view particularly provincial, in that there has been a lot of publicity recently for the view that foreign law and foreign law concepts like *droit moral* should be considered by U.S. courts in deciding U.S. cases. For example, Justice Kennedy of the U.S. Supreme Court has been quoted as espousing his belief "that by invoking foreign law, the United States Supreme Court sends an implicit message to the rest of the democratic world that our society shares its values. 'The European courts, in particular the transnational courts, have been somewhat concerned, and some feel demeaned, that we did not cite their decisions with more regularity. . . . They cite ours all the time. And, basically, they were saying, "Why should we cite yours if you don't cite ours?"'" (Jeffrey Toobin, "Swing Shift: How Anthony Kennedy's passion for foreign law could change the Supreme Court," *The New Yorker*, Sept. 12, 2005, at 50.)

Schwenck appears not to be aware of, or at least not to consider important, such influential cases as *Turner Entertainment Company v. Huston*, CA Versailles [France], civ. Ch., Dec. 19, 1994, which held that colorization of a filmmaker's film print constituted a violation of *droit moral*. To me, this provincialism explains why Schwenck and, apparently, Dunstable have failed to understand that an argument based on *droit moral* would have tilted the scales of justice in Point's favor in the arbitration.

FS April 6, YR-1

REPORT OF DR. RUTH SCHWENCK[8]

I am providing this report to set out my expert opinion concerning the claims plaintiff Point has made against her attorney in the matter of *Point v. Dunstable.*

I am a professor of law at Basing School of Law, Stoke University located in South Kensington, Nita, which is where I received my JD in YR-44. I have been a tenured professor there since YR-34. My main field of teaching is Professional Responsibility, but I have also developed a course that I teach to undergraduates entitled "Law on Stage and Screen," a fairly light, easy-to-digest introduction to the law from an entertainment perspective. I have an honorary PhD in law from the University of Sloane in Despard-super-Mare, U.K. (hence my honorific "Dr."), which I received because of my work over the years encouraging prelaw undergraduates to do a semester abroad in law studies. (Yes, people always ask me if that is really the name of the city where Sloane is located. It is. "Mare" is pronounced MEHR.)

I have published two books and numerous articles in my two fields of interest. The main ones are:

- *Everyday Ethics: A Practical Guide for Lawyers* (Stoke Univ. Press YR-15)

- *Making Lawyers Real on Stage & Screen* (Sloane Univ. Press YR-16)

- "How to Recognize and Resolve 'Apparent' Conflicts of Interest," 14 Basing L. Rev. 136 (YR-16)

- "'Diligence' Under the New ABA Model Rules," *Nita Bar Ass'n News* (March YR-8)

- "Fred Thompson: Lawyer-Actor or Actor-Lawyer?," *New York Times* (January 9, YR-7)

I have testified four times as an expert witness in the field of professional responsibility and legal ethics. In all cases, I testified for the attorney-defendant. All four cases were malpractice actions. None of the cases involved IP issues similar to those in Point's claim against MajorFilms. Instead, all were of a more "garden variety" form of legal malpractice involving more traditional contract- or tort-based claims for recovery.

In preparing for this case, I studied the pleadings, the depositions, the arbitration decision in *Point and MajorFilms, Inc.,* the documents exchanged by the parties, and the expert report of Frederic Sullivan. I also refamiliarized myself with the prevailing standards of conduct of attorneys practicing in Nita by reading reports of court decisions in legal

8. If played by a male witness, Rufus Schwenck.

malpractice cases litigated in Nita courts and the reported decisions of the Nita Bar Association's Ethics Adjudication Board in cases involving attorney disciplinary actions.

As I understand the plaintiff's claims in the present action against Dunstable, they are based on three alleged failures to abide by ethical standards in the conduct of the litigation, which the plaintiff claims can be used to assess whether Dunstable met or exceeded the prevailing standard of care in legal representation. My professional opinion is that there is no merit to any of the plaintiff's claims. Dunstable neither breached his ethical obligations nor failed in any way properly to pursue the plaintiff's suit against MajorFilms. It is also my professional opinion that MajorFilms's position in the underlying arbitration was a sound one and accordingly that Dunstable's strategy for countering that position was correctly analyzed and presented.

1. Alleged Failure to Abide by Client's Desired Goals

Point complains that she wanted Dunstable to assert a claim under the doctrine of *droit moral* to buttress her claim based on breach of contract, and that his failure to do so a) was a substantial factor in causing her loss in the arbitration, and b) improperly disregarded one of her overall goals for the litigation, i.e., to make a case for increased use of *droit moral* as an avenue of relief for artists complaining of harm to their works or reputation.

First, as to the causation factor, I see no way that the history of the arbitration proceedings supports a claim that <u>the absence of the term *droit moral* itself, in *haec verba*</u>, can be linked to Point's loss. Dunstable argued both the legal and the equitable grounds on which Point's claim against MajorFilms should be sustained. The equitable argument included the claim that MajorFilms's change in the film unfairly and improperly altered Point's artistic work and her artistic message. That being the case, the arbitrators were free to make a full or partial award to Point on this equitable basis, which would have been the full equivalent of an award based on *droit moral*. The fact that they did not make such an award shows that they were not convinced by her *facts* or her *legal interpretation of the agreement*—as opposed to not convinced by Dunstable's alleged failure to use the *terminology* of *droit moral*.

Second, as to whether Dunstable should have used the term *droit moral* itself to advance Point's goal of increasing support for *droit moral*, there are three answers.

- As recited above, the non-use of the term was not the problem. The difficulty Point had was that her *facts* did not support her claim. Thus, since using the term *droit moral* would not have changed the result, the use likewise would not have increased the social, jurisprudential, or legal support for the use of the concept in U.S. law.

- Under NRPC 1.2, Scope of Representation and Allocation of Authority Between Client and Lawyer, the dividing line between the "objectives of [the] representation," which generally a client controls, albeit in consultation with the attorney, and the legal "means by which [the objectives] are to be pursued," which generally the attorney controls (again, in consultation with the client), cannot be drawn with absolute precision. Here, Dunstable fought hard for Point's right to have her work presented without change. That is the essence, as I understand it, of the leg of *droit moral* on which Point is relying. But Dunstable also had to devise the best strategy to try to win the best result he could. By my review of the course of the proceedings below, he did that.

- Viewed another way, Point's goal of promoting *droit moral* was inconsistent with, and worked against, her other goal of obtaining relief (financial and other) in the arbitration. As Dunstable told her at one point, the use of a foreign-law concept might not only not *persuade* the arbitrators but might do much worse—it might *dissuade* them from seeing the strength of her breach-of-contract and equitable case. Despite what Point and Sullivan say, *droit moral* is *not* a concept recognized in U.S. law, except for the anomalous *Gilliam* case in the Second Circuit, which most authorities view as an aberration. And the passage of the few laws that resemble *droit moral* (only California and New York have them), and of VARA in the federal statutes, only emphasizes how hostile U.S. law is to the concept. Since these three statutes do not provide *droit moral* type protection to filmmakers but only to the plastic arts and photography, they demonstrate that U.S. legislators do not accept the idea that a *droit moral* type of protection should be expanded beyond the limited coverage of the statutes.

2. Alleged Failure to Investigate Arbitrators' and Expert Witness's Backgrounds

Point asserts that Dunstable should have done more in-depth investigation of the backgrounds of arbitrators Primus, Dupple, and Noble, and of MajorFilms's expert witness, Edwin Merill. According to Point, such investigation would have disclosed the following:

- Dupple had a history of disagreements with Point's expert Frederic Sullivan, which Point claims could have affected Dupple's view of Sullivan's testimony and/or of Point's case.

- Dupple had once worked as a partner in the New York law firm that regularly represents MajorFilms in matters on the East Coast.

- Noble was favorably disposed to the use of *droit moral* as a basis for recovery; Point claims that knowledge of this could have guided her and Dunstable in the presentation of her case, to feature *droit moral* more specifically and by name.

- Primus and Merill had a closer relationship than they described in disclosing their prior acquaintance, giving rise to Point's suspicion that Primus's view of Merill as her "mentor" could have influenced Primus's view of the evidence.

All of these claims allude to NRPC 1.1, Competence, and/or 1.3, Diligence, which have been interpreted by the ethics decisions in Nita and other jurisdictions as including the duty to investigate thoroughly in preparation of a case. However, all of the consequences that Point surmises are purely speculative. She has not cited any conduct or comment at the arbitration that supplies proof beyond this speculation. The supposed conflict of interest posed by Dupple's one-time association with the New York firm of Oakapple & Murgatroyd is a good example—there has been no showing that Dupple ever worked on a MajorFilms matter at O&M, that he had any continuing close connection with anyone at O&M who handles MajorFilms's matters, or indeed that he even knew that O&A represents MajorFilms.

Litigation proceedings are always contentious and adversarial—it is the nature of the setting. But it does not follow that every small flaw in the sanctity of the proceedings will lead inevitably to adverse effects on the party concerned. In my opinion, this observation disposes of Point's claims under NRPC 1.1 and 1.3. Without proof—direct or circumstantial—to show that she suffered actual harm, there is no ground for recovery on these claims.

3. Alleged Failure to Communicate Adequately with the Client

Finally, under NRPC 1.4, "Communication," Point asserts that Dunstable was required to communicate with her more fully about certain aspects of the litigation. In many respects, this claim overlaps with the first two, in that she contends he should have disclosed more information to her about the arbitrators—or at least told her the limited extent of his inquiry so that she could investigate further on her own, that he should have discussed with her more fully the ramifications of accepting Primus as chair even after her relationship with Merill was disclosed, and that he should have been more forthcoming in advising her why, and to what extent, he decided at each juncture not to assert her claim specifically under *droit moral.*

Other alleged failures to communicate are separate: that he should have told her she would be at risk for the arbitration costs and fees, that his description of his handling of a previous similar case (*Samuels v. KZBT*) was misleading, and that he should have returned her phone calls in September YR-3 when finalizing the demand for arbitration.

All of these claims of mis- or nonfeasance are, in my view, minor and reflect nothing more than the inevitable dissatisfaction of the losing party in litigation. The expression, "Take *shoulda, coulda, woulda* and four dollars and get yourself a latte at Starbucks," pretty accurately describes the basic response that such claims engender. This may seem harsh to the nonlawyer, but the fact is that in the heat of the fight, when split-second decisions have to be made, we expect of lawyers only the reasonable, not the utmost, efforts when we analyze how well they communicated with the client. Dunstable met this standard in this case.

4. Alleged Incorrect Strategy to Counter MajorFilms's Defense

Finally, Point seems to make an overarching complaint that Dunstable incorrectly handled her suit against MajorFilms, specifically, that using *droit moral* could have overcome some of the contract interpretation difficulties that Point faced in pressing her claims. Again, as in the complaint about Dunstable's alleged failure to "lobby" for *droit moral* through the platform of the arbitration, it is my opinion that Point's contention elevates form over substance.

Whether Dunstable argued breach of contract, equitable grounds for relief, or *droit moral*, the question the arbitrators were going to answer remained the same: did the agreement give Point rights that MajorFilms violated, or instead was MajorFilms acting within *its* rights under the agreement when it colorized the balloon. From my familiarity with the doctrine of *droit moral*, which I have studied both in my work on Law in Drama and also in preparation for this testimony, *droit moral* does not change the analysis of paragraph 7(a) and (b) of the agreement:

- Was the change that MajorFilms made "minor?" If it was, MajorFilms acted within its rights.

- In the alternative, did the change "alter the essential artistic aspects" of the film? If it did not, then MajorFilms likewise acted within its rights.

My opinion is reinforced by the plausibility of MajorFilms's explanation of its purpose and theory for the change in the balloon's color: to suggest that although the world was tilting towards a kind of homogenized society, nevertheless there was still hope for color and differentiation. The balloon had lost a lot of color since the 1950s, but not all. For an audience based in the U.S., which is a comparatively "upbeat" country (as contrasted with France, which takes a more jaundiced view of life), MajorFilms made a sound decision in modifying the film as it did. It is therefore not surprising to me that the arbitrators found that MajorFilms had the correct side of the case.

Dunstable met these arguments as best he could with Point's testimony and expert witness Sullivan's supporting views. However, I see no way in which *droit moral* would have strengthened Point's case.

For all these reasons, my opinion is that Dunstable met the standard of care expected of attorneys practicing in Nita in his field.

I am being paid for my time spent in developing and rendering advice and consultation at my standard expert witness consultation rate of $350 an hour as well as for my time in court appearances and any deposition testimony at my standard expert-witness appearance rate of $450 an hour. From my familiarity with attorneys and academics who serve as expert witnesses in similar matters and factual settings, these rates are in the range of experts in my field who have experience and reputations comparable to mine. To date, I have accrued fees of $5,250, representing fifteen hours of consultation.

Ruth Schwenck

Dated: March 9, YR-1

EXHIBITS

Exhibit 1

"Film Forum" Newspaper Clipping

blackBOOK

Places That Still Matter

Film Forum

Against all odds, this is the little art house cinema that can—showing everything from crazy cool Korean kitsch to neorealist masterpieces.

Buried in an unnamed neighborhood, just south of the Village and west of SoHo, on the block where Houston Street narrows into a conduit for the West Side Highway, Film Forum is a city treasure.

A three-screen neo-Deco establishment, as well as an autonomous nonprofit with a multimillion-dollar budget, Film Forum had little more than a projector and 50 folding chairs when it was founded by Peter Feinstein and Sandy Miller in 1970 in an Upper West Side loft. Two years later Karen Cooper, then what she calls "an all-around slave" at a short-lived film publication, dropped by and was handed the business. (Those were the days...) She moved operations downtown, first to an exceedingly snug off-off-off-Broadway theater, and then to a relatively capacious former garage near the entrance to the Holland Tunnel.

Cooper established the theater as the New York home for documentaries, American independents, and innovative Europeans, premièring and reviving work by such then near-unknowns as Werner Herzog, Wim Wenders, and Chantal Akerman. Along with Mike Maggiore, Cooper still selects Film Forum's new work, while Bruce Goldstein—who has run retrospectives and restorations since those early days—brings in some pop showmanship and film history. (For 1988's Gimmick-o-Rama, he wired every third seat with a motorized buzzer to provide "Percepto!": the full sensory experience required for William Castle's 1959 Vincent Price thriller *The Tingler*.)

No other New York theater has Film Forum's range—a mix of arcane and popular, avant-garde and retro. The venue has opened everything from Matthew Barney's fantasies and the 2007 Iraq War documentary *No End in Sight* to the original Japanese-language version of *Godzilla*. And no other theater has the power of Film Forum's imprimatur. Miramax acquired Jennie Livingston's 1991 *Paris Is Burning*, a documentary of Manhattan's drag balls, after it packed the place for six months. For the cognoscenti a Film Forum booking simply gives street cred. Last fall the theatrical première of Todd Haynes's Bob Dylan biopic *I'm Not There* set a house record.

As a venue, Film Forum exerts an influence far beyond Manhattan. Not only does a screening there ensure national attention but the theater's inventive programming has been imitated by media centers across the nation. Goldstein's festivals have created new varieties of film noir and more or less invented pre-Code Hollywood cinema as a genre. And thanks to his 3-D series, Film Forum is the only theater in New York capable of fifties-style 3-D projection. When Martin Scorsese purchased a number of vintage 3-D prints a few years back, he had to come down to Houston Street to screen them.

Things haven't always been peachy. There was an eviction in 1989, after which Cooper resettled the theater at its current industrial-chic digs in a former printing plant, the fancifully ascetic interior of which has been deftly carved into three tunnels of about 150 seats each. (The sight lines are good, the recently reupholstered seats are... cozy.) Cooper asked her architect for Brancusi meets Pee-wee's playhouse, and that's what she got. In the lobby there's a kidney-shaped counter and a 19th-century hand-cranked Mutoscope showing flip book movies.

Fans include Ethan Hawke, Parker Posey, Lou Reed, Laurie Anderson, Nicole Kidman, the Coen brothers, and late greats Susan Sontag and Fay Wray. Wallace Shawn has been spotted here, too. Even the seats are Boldfaced Names. Patrons have dedicated them to movies (*Roger & Me*, *High Anxiety*) and to such screen icons as Louise Brooks and Betty Boop. Diane Keaton dedicated one to her cat, Buster—there's one named for Buster Keaton, too.

And the snacks! *New York Times* critic A. O. Scott said Film Forum has "the best movie-house popcorn in Manhattan," and the late French philosopher Jacques Derrida told *Time* magazine "I love this banana bread," referring to one of the concession stand's confections.

I've discovered—or rediscovered—more great things at Film Forum than I could ever possibly list. I never much cared for Woody Allen's *Manhattan*, for example, until I saw it there last summer. As I left the theater, it all came together for me: wise-guy one-liners, Astaire-Rogers music, neurotic obsessions, and gorgeous black and white. New York's sooty glamour and a passionate love of movies. Diane Keaton's seat and Wally Shawn in the audience: Film Forum. *At 209 W. Houston St.; 212-727-8110; filmforum.org.*

—J. HOBERMAN *recently celebrated his 30th year as a movie critic at* The Village Voice. *His ten books include* The Magic Hour: Film at Fin de Siecle.

Exhibit 2

"Indie Film Companies Join Forces" Newspaper Clipping

Indie Film Companies Join Forces

Two well-known names in the world of independent and international film releasing have joined forces, forming a single company that its principals said would make them "the biggest of the little guys." On Wednesday, Kino International, which has helped introduce American audiences to foreign filmmakers like **Wong Kar-wai** and **Michael Haneke**, and Lorber HT Digital, which has handled art-house releases like "The Sun" by **Alexander Sokurov**, said they had merged into Kino-Lorber Inc., which will be run jointly by the Kino founder **Donald Krim** and **Richard Lorber**, the Lorber HT Digital chief executive. Under the new company, the Kino and Lorber banners will still handle their own theatrical and home video releases.

Exhibit 3

Distributorship Agreement (Not Executed)

Distributorship Agreement

JOSÉPHINE POINT ("Artist") and MajorFilms, Inc. ("Distributor") (collectively, the "Parties"), for good and valuable consideration and intending to be legally bound, do hereby covenant and agree:

1. Artist is the maker of short-feature films (the "Films"), which she wishes to have placed for showing in film festivals, art theaters, and public television broadcasts (collectively, the "Desired Placements").
2. Distributor desires to assist Artist with such Desired Placements, in return for receiving such rental or screening fees as Distributor is able to negotiate with the screening entity.
3. Distributor shall bear all costs of advertising, promotion, and screening.
4. Artist shall be entitled to receive: in Years 1-2 of this Agreement, Fifteen Per Cent (15%); in Years 3-4, Twenty-Five Per Cent (25%); and in Year 5, Thirty-Five Per Cent (35%) of any rental or screening fees paid to Distributor for showing of the Films.
5. The term of this Agreement shall be Five (5) Years from date of execution.
6. Artist shall retain all copyrights in the Films.
7. Distributor shall have the right to make such alterations to the Films as in its opinion are necessary for the successful marketing and placement of the Films.
8. This Agreement shall be governed by the law of the State of Nita. Any dispute arising under this Agreement shall be submitted for binding decision to the Nita Arbitration Forum, under the Forum's rules and procedures. By stipulation of the parties, NAF shall be required to apply and follow the law of the State of Nita.
9. This Agreement encompasses the entire agreement of the parties; supersedes all previous understandings and agreements between the Parties, whether oral or written; and may be amended only by a writing signed by both Artist and Distributor.

[not executed]
Artist

[not executed]
Distributor

Executed this _____ day of ___________________, YR-4

Exhibit 4

Representation Agreement

LAW OFFICES OF STANLEY DUNSTABLE LLC

© ™ ®

REPRESENTATION AGREEMENT

I hereby retain the law firm of Stanley Dunstable, LLC, to represent me with respect to all aspects of representation of my interests in relation to a proposed Distributorship Agreement (the "Agreement") between me and MajorFilms, Inc ("Distributor"), including but not limited to negotiation of the terms of the Agreement and prosecution or defense of any claims that may arise thereunder.

I agree that I will pay all hourly fees incurred by Stanley Dunstable, LLC, in his representation of my interest as aforesaid, and I acknowledge that I have been informed that his current billing rate is $400 per hour.

I agree that I am responsible for all reasonable and necessary costs and expenses incurred in the negotiation of the Agreement and in the investigation, prosecution, or defense of any claims that may arise thereunder.

I further understand and agree that by this agreement, Stanley Dunstable, LLC, is not committed in any way to proceed with any lawsuit and has the right at any time to determine that it is not appropriate to continue to handle my case.

I understand that all reasonable and necessary expenses incurred in the negotiation of the Agreement and in any prosecution or defense of any claims that may arise thereunder must be paid by me, regardless of the outcome of the negotiations or any lawsuit.

By my signature hereto, I acknowledge that I have read and understand the terms of this Representation Agreement and that I have received a copy of it.

/s/ *Joséphine Point*
Joséphine Point

Dated: March 15, YR-4

Exhibit 5

Distributed Agreement (Not Executed, Highlighted)

Distributorship Agreement

JOSÉPHINE POINT ("Artist") and MajorFilms, Inc. ("Distributor") (collectively, the "Parties"), for good and valuable consideration and intending to be legally bound, do hereby covenant and agree:

1. Artist is the maker of short-feature films (the "Films"), which she wishes to have placed for showing in film festivals, art theaters, and public television broadcasts (collectively, the "Desired Placements").
2. Distributor desires to assist Artist with such Desired Placements, in return for receiving such rental or screening fees as Distributor is able to negotiate with the screening entity.
3. Distributor shall bear all costs of advertising, promotion, and screening.
4. Artist shall be entitled to receive: in Years 1-2 of this Agreement, Fifteen Per Cent (15%); in Years 3-4, Twenty-Five Per Cent (25%); and in Year 5, Thirty-Five Per Cent (35%) of any rental or screening fees paid to Distributor for showing of the Films.
5. The term of this Agreement shall be Five (5) Years from date of execution.
6. Artist shall retain all copyrights in the Films and all other artist's rights except as otherwise provided herein.
7. Distributor shall have the right at all times to make (a) minor alterations to the Films and (b) such other alterations to the Films as in its opinion are necessary for the successful marketing and placement of the Films. However, no alterations may be made under (b) hereof unless (i) the Artist has agreed to such alterations (which agreement shall not be unreasonably withheld) or (ii) if the Artist does not so agree, the dispute has first been submitted to the Dispute Panel of the Nita Volunteer Lawyers for the Arts (the "VLA Panel"). The VLA Panel's decision shall be final and binding upon Artist and Distributor.
8. The parties agree that, due to the impracticability of ascertaining the amount of actual damages caused by a material breach of paragraphs 6 and/or 7 of this Agreement, Distributor shall pay to Artist, as liquidated damages, Ten Thousand Dollars ($10,000) for each and any such breach that is found under the dispute resolution clause (paragraph 9 hereof), as liquidated damages and not as a penalty. The Parties further agree that nothing in this paragraph 8 is intended to limit Artist's right to obtain injunctive or such other relief as may be appropriate.
9. This Agreement shall be governed by the law of the State of Nita. Any dispute arising under this Agreement shall be submitted for binding decision to the Nita Arbitration Forum, under the Forum's rules and procedures. By stipulation of the parties, NAF shall be required to apply and follow the law of the State of Nita.
10. This Agreement encompasses the entire agreement of the Parties; supersedes all previous understandings and agreements between the Parties, whether oral or written; and may be amended only by a writing signed by both Artist and Distributor.

[not executed] ____________ Artist

[not executed] ____________ Distributor

Executed this _____ day of _________________, YR-4

[Case File Note: language changed from Ex. 3 is shaded here, for ease of reference.]

Exhibit 6

Letter from Joséphine Point to MajorFilms, Dated May 23, YR-4

Ms. Mabel Swoop
MajorFilms, Inc.
92 Barrow St
New York NY 10014

23 May YR-4

RE: Point—MajorFilms Distributorship Agreement

Dear Mabel:

Thank you for agreeing to allow me to add some minor "tweaks" to the alterations provision in the draft of the Agreement you sent me last month. You and I talked these over on the phone, so I believe we are on the same page concerning the language in paragraphs 6 and 7. As we discussed, my main concern is to have language that assures me of my ability to protect the essential artistic aspects of the Films.

I also added, as we discussed, a fairly standard form of liquidated damages clause, since we know how hard it would be for me to demonstrate or measure actual dollar damages.

Trusting you find the agreement acceptable in all respects, I look forward to receiving it back with your execution; I will then send you a conformed copy.

Let's all go to the movies!

Yours,

/s/ Joséphine Point

Encl: [copy of Ex. 5, unexecuted]

cc: Stanley Dunstable, Esq. (w/ encl.)

Exhibit 7

Distributorship Agreement (Executed, Highlighted)

Distributorship Agreement

JOSÉPHINE POINT ("Artist") and MajorFilms, Inc. ("Distributor") (collectively, the "Parties"), for good and valuable consideration and intending to be legally bound, do hereby covenant and agree:

1. Artist is the maker of short-feature films (the "Films"), which she wishes to have placed for showing in film festivals, art theaters, and public television broadcasts (collectively, the "Desired Placements") in any appropriate placements within, but limited to, the United States.

2. Distributor desires to assist Artist with such Desired Placements, in return for receiving such rental or screening fees as Distributor is able to negotiate with the screening entity.

3. Distributor shall bear all costs of advertising, promotion, and screening.

4. Artist shall be entitled to receive: in Years 1-2 of this Agreement, Fifteen Per Cent (15%); in Years 3-4, Twenty-Five Per Cent (25%); and in Year 5, Thirty-Five Per Cent (35%) of any rental or screening fees paid to Distributor for showing of the Films.

5. The term of this Agreement shall be Five (5) Years from date of execution.

6. Artist shall retain all copyrights in the Films and all other artist's rights except as otherwise provided herein.

MS JP 7. Notwithstanding Artist's copyrights / Lanham Act rights / rights of publicity, Distributor shall have the right at all times to make (a) minor alterations to the Films and (b) such other alterations to the Films as in its opinion are necessary for the successful marketing and placement of the Films. *MS JP* However, no alterations affecting the essential artistic aspects of the Films may be made under (b) hereof unless (i) the Artist has agreed to such alterations (which agreement shall not be unreasonably withheld) or (ii) if the Artist does not so agree, the dispute has first been submitted to the Dispute Panel of the Nita Volunteer Lawyers for the Arts (the "VLA Panel"). The VLA Panel's decision shall be final and binding upon Artist and Distributor.

8. The parties agree that, due to the impracticability of ascertaining the amount of actual damages caused by a material breach of paragraphs 6 and/or 7 of this Agreement, Distributor shall pay to Artist, as liquidated damages, Ten Thousand Dollars ($10,000) for each and any such breach that is found under the dispute resolution clause (paragraph 9 hereof), as liquidated damages and not as a penalty. The Parties further agree that nothing in this paragraph 8 is intended to limit Artist's right to obtain injunctive or such other relief as may be appropriate.

9. This Agreement shall be governed by the law of the State of Nita. Any dispute arising under this Agreement shall be submitted for binding decision to the Nita Arbitration Forum, under the Forum's rules and procedures. By stipulation of the parties, NAF shall be required to apply and follow the law of the State of Nita.

10. This Agreement encompasses the entire agreement of the Parties; supersedes all previous understandings and agreements between the Parties, whether oral or written, and may be amended only by a writing signed by both Artist and Distributor.

/s/ Joséphine Point	*/s/ Mabel Swoop, President*
Artist	Distributor

Executed this *6th* day of *June*, YR-4

[Case File Note: language changed from Ex. 5 is shaded here, for ease of reference.]

Exhibit 8

Letter from MajorFilms, Inc. to Joséphine Point, Dated June 6, YR-4

MajorFilms, Inc.
92 Barrow Street
New York, NY 10014

June 6, YR-4

Ms. Joséphine Point
91 Mansfield St.
Nita City, NI 02220

RE: Point/MajorFilms Distributorship Agreement

Dear Joséphine:

I am delighted we have been able to reach agreement on our distributorship arrangement. I reviewed your additional paragraphs 6 through 8 and, understanding that they are not intended to create any undue delays or barriers to our successful marketing and placement of your films, have executed the Agreement. As you and I discussed after I received your revision, I added the two phrases to paragraph 7 that we discussed to clarify the alteration provisions. The phrases are underlined and initialed by me to show the revisions—please add your initials as well, then send us a fully conformed copy for our files.

All right now, let's do some good!

Yours,

/s/ Mabel Swoop
President

P.S. I talked over the changes with George, and he wanted to be sure we were not forbidden under the new terms you added from finding the best ways to suit your films to U.S. audiences. I told him you and I had agreed on that.

Encl: [copy of Exhibit 7 executed by MajorFilms]

Exhibit 9

Joséphine Point Notes, Dated June 13, YR-4

13.6.YR-4
Called Dunst. to review MF's june 6 lttr § redraft

2 changes OK

Initial margins — execute and return to MF
$.$

Zut! Yeah!

Awesome

I think I'm going to

$.$.$.$ be famous!

Exhibit 10

Sundance Festival Newspaper Clippings

Sundance, Thinking Indie, Tries to Hone Its Artsy Edge

By BROOKS BARNES

LOS ANGELES — Sundance, under new leadership, is trying to tilt risky.

The programmers of the Sundance Film Festival on Wednesday announced a schedule of competition films that at least in their view, reflect no particular current in independent cinema except one: the artier the better.

"We really tried to hunker down and make some hard decisions," said John Cooper, the festival's new director. "We tried not to be wishy-washy about what is independent, which I know has been a criticism in the past. We weren't going to be swayed by the marketability of a film."

Mr. Cooper, who took over in February following the departure of Geoffrey Gilmore, who held the director job for 19 years, pointed to selected pictures like "Blue Valentine," a raw portrait of an unhappy marriage from a relatively unknown director, Derek Cianfrance. "Howl," a look at the young Allen Ginsberg's creation of his groundbreaking poem, is another selection that "risks against commerciality," Mr. Cooper said.

Hollywood is likely to debate that one — "Howl," directed by Rob Epstein and Jeffrey Friedman ("The Celluloid Closet"), stars the highly promotable James Franco — but "Night Catches Us" is safely in the risky category. The film, from the first-time director Tanya Hamilton, is an ambitious period piece set in 1976

Sundance Festival, With a New Leader, Tries to Hone Its Artsy Edge

Philadelphia; a young man returns to the race-torn neighborhood where he had come of age during the Black Power movement.

The festival, both a pre-eminent showcase for American cinema and a free-wheeling bazaar for movie executives, is scheduled for Jan. 21 to 31 in Park City, Utah, and several surrounding towns. (A full list of the competition films can be found at nytimes.com/carpetbagger.)

A weakening independent movie market, particularly when it comes to the financing of art-house pictures, did not affect the number of submissions, as some festival watchers had predicted, perhaps because it takes so long to make a film that some of the deals for this year's submissions may have been struck before the credit crunch. Feature-length submissions from the United States totaled 1,920 — a slight increase after falling by 6 percent last year — while foreign submissions climbed to 1,804.

There were 113 features selected (including noncompetition films still to be announced), down from 118 last year.

Sundance has always made risky selections. Last year's grand jury prize and audience award in the United States dramatic competition went to "Precious: Based on the Novel 'Push' by Sapphire," about a 300-pound Harlem teenager who suffers extreme abuse from both parents. Hardly a marketing cakewalk, although it has been doing quite well in its early weeks of limited release and is frequently cited as an Oscar contender.

But as independent film boomed over the last decade, the festival at times showed a willingness to give premiere slots as favors to studios or put too much emphasis on advance buzz from sales agents and scouts when making selections. Mr. Cooper, along with Sundance's founder, Robert Redford, is trying to address such criticism and show that the festival is not rigid in its thinking.

"It is not our place to decide what will be shown a year from now in theaters," Mr. Redford said in a statement. Mr. Redford, who Mr. Cooper said had become more of a "silent partner" in recent years, has come back into planning for the festival full time.

A swing toward art over commerce is perhaps inevitable given the market. Over the last two years studios have folded specialty divisions (Warner Independent, Paramount Vantage) or scaled them back drastically (Miramax). Outside the studio system, financing has become extremely difficult to obtain due to the credit crisis and recession.

"We have a film industry in great evolutionary flux, but we can't think too much about that," Mr. Cooper said. "We have to stay on mission and let the industry sort itself out."

Among other changes, Mr. Cooper opted to end the tradition of having one opening-night film. Instead the festival will dive straight into the competition with one narrative, one documentary and one shorts program playing on Day 1. This year's installment will also have a new section highlighting innovative work in "low- and no-budget filmmaking." The section, called Next, will include eight United States films. (Selections will be announced on Thursday.)

Still, this is Sundance. A-list names like George Clooney and Brad Pitt may not be on the roster, but there are still plenty of well-known people involved with selected films to make for a buzzy festival.

Kristen Stewart, the 19-year-old co-star of the "Twilight" blockbusters, plays a New Orleans stripper in "Welcome to the Rileys," which also stars James Gandolfini as a damaged businessman. Mr. Cooper noted that Ms. Stewart also has a noncompetition entry: in "The Runaways," directed by Floria Sigismondi, Ms. Stewart plays a young Joan Jett.

Peppering the selection list are films with bold-face names like Ryan Gosling, Michelle Williams, Natalie Portman, Rainn Wilson, Edie Falco, Mary-Louise Parker and Jon Hamm. In the still-grinding-away department is Piper Laurie, who plays a grandmother in "Hesher," about a mysterious troublemaker who moves in with a family trying to cope with devastating loss.

Multiple films came from actors turned directors. Leading the pack is Mark Ruffalo ("You Can Count on Me") with the quirky drama "Sympathy for Delicious," about a newly paralyzed D.J. who gets more than he bargained for when he seeks out the world of faith healing. Written by Christopher Thornton, it stars Orlando Bloom and Juliette Lewis, among others.

With documentaries, Mr. Cooper said, efforts were made to avoid thematic gridlock. So favorite topics like environmental calamity and war are represented but by fewer entries than in years past. "Gas Land," directed by Josh Fox, looks at the downside — dying livestock, toxic streams — of the natural gas drilling craze; "Restrepo," directed by Sebastian Junger and Tim Hetherington, focuses on the war in Afghanistan.

On the lighter side are selections like "Joan Rivers: a Piece of Work," directed by Ricki Stern and Annie Sundberg, and "Smash His Camera," the story of a reviled paparazzo from the director Leon Gast. "The documentary selections this year are much more nontraditional in style — more nonfiction storytelling versus the standard format," Mr. Cooper said.

John Cooper looking at the board where he and his team schedule Sundance festival screenings.

The Carpetbagger

Melena Ryzik and team cover all the news and nonsense of the film awards season:

nytimes.com/movies

A new leader plans a festival, along with its founder, Robert Redford.

ONLINE: MORE ON SUNDANCE

Additional news, features and videos about the Sundance Film Festival:

nytimes.com/movies

'HOWL' James Franco portrays the young Allen Ginsberg as he is creating his signature poem.

'WELCOME TO THE RILEYS' James Gandolfini as a businessman and Kristen Stewart as a stripper.

'RESTREPO' A scene from the film directed by Sebastian Junger and Tim Hetherington.

Exhibit 11A

Demand for Arbitration (Draft)

NITA ARBITRATION FORUM

DRAFT 9/5/YR-3 NAF File YR-3-

Demand for Arbitration

Claimant Joséphine Point hereby demands arbitration proceedings against Respondent MajorFilms, Inc. arising out of and pertaining to the attached Distributorship Agreement between the parties (Ex. A), pursuant to paragraph 9 thereof.

In support of her Demand, Claimant asserts that Respondent has breached the Agreement by:

1. Altering Claimant's film *What Red Balloon?* ("the Film") in derogation of Claimant's right to object to such alteration pursuant to paragraph 7(b) of the said Agreement;
2. Failing to present an unaltered version of the Film to the YR-3 Sundance Festival, as agreed by the parties; and
3. Misrepresenting Claimant's artistic work by altering the Film without Claimant's consent.

Clamant has been harmed by the said breaches by:

1. Damage to her professional and artistic reputation;
2. Failure of the Film to win any award or mention at the said Festival; and
3. Such other damages as Claimant shall prove at the arbitration proceedings.

WHEREFORE, Claimant demands monetary damages in an amount to be proved at arbitration; the entry of an injunction barring further alteration of, or dissemination of an altered form of, the Film; and all such other relief available to her at law or in equity.

Att: Ex. A [cc. of Ex. 7 of Case File] ______________________ Attorney for Claimant

Exhibit 11B

Demand for Arbitration (Signed)

NITA ARBITRATION FORUM

In re Joséphine Point, Claimant
- and -
MajorFilms, Inc., Respondent

NAF File YR-3-

Demand for Arbitration

Claimant Joséphine Point hereby demands arbitration proceedings against Respondent MajorFilms, Inc. arising out of and pertaining to the attached Distributorship Agreement between the parties (Ex. A), pursuant to paragraph 9 thereof.

In support of her Demand, Claimant asserts that Respondent has breached the Agreement by:

1. Altering Claimant's film *What Red Balloon?* ("the Film") in derogation of Claimant's right to object to such alteration pursuant to paragraph 7(b) of the said Agreement;
2. Failing to present an unaltered version of the Film to the YR-3 Sundance Festival ("the Festival"), as agreed by the parties; and
3. Misrepresenting Claimant's artistic work by altering the Film without Claimant's consent.

Clamant has been harmed by the said breaches by:

1. Damage to her professional and artistic reputation;
2. Failure of the Film to win any award or mention at the Festival; and
3. Such other damages as Claimant shall prove at the arbitration proceedings.

WHEREFORE, Claimant demands monetary damages in an amount to be proved at arbitration; the entry of an injunction barring further alteration of, or dissemination of an altered form of, the Film; and all such other relief available to her at law or in equity.

Dated and Filed: October 2, YR-3
Att: Ex. A [cc. of Ex. 7 of Case File]

/s/ *Stanley Dunstable*
Stanley Dunstable, Attorney for Claimant

Exhibit 11C

Reply to Demand for Arbitration (Signed)

NITA ARBITRATION FORUM

In re Joséphine Point, Claimant
- and -
MajorFilms, Inc., Respondent

NAF File YR-3-14850

Reply to Demand for Arbitration

Respondent MajorFilms, Inc., by its undersigned attorney, hereby replies to the Demand for Arbitration of Claimant Joséphine Point:

The Demand is denied in its entirety.

Dated and Filed: October 10, YR-3

s/ Joseph Flume
Joseph Flume, Attorney for Respondent

Exhibit 12

Arbitration Decision

NITA ARBITRATION FORUM

In re Joséphine Point, Claimant
- and -
MajorFilms, Inc., Respondent

NAF File YR-3-14850

Arbitration Decision

The undersigned arbitration panel, after hearings held November 20-21, YR-3, and upon due consideration of the parties' testimonies and evidence submitted, hereby rules in favor of

MajorFilms, Inc., Respondent

and directs that

Joséphine Point, Claimant

shall pay to Nita Arbitration Forum the Arbitration costs and fees in the amount of

Twenty-Seven Thousand Dollars and No Cents ($27,000.00).

Dated: February 29, YR-2

/s/ *Emily Primus*	/s/ *H.D. Dupple*	
Panel Chairperson	Panel Arbitrator	Panel Arbitrator

DISSENTING VOTE:
I hereby note my dissenting vote to the Panel's decision. In my view, the doctrine of *droit moral* provides the protections and relief that Claimant sought in these proceedings, and while Claimant's case was not presented as founded on *droit moral* specifically, nevertheless the proofs presented raised the issue sufficiently and it should have been considered.

/s/ *Tertius Noble*
Panel Arbitrator

Exhibit 13A

Telephone Message Slip, Dated September 10, YR-3

LAW OFFICES OF STANLEY DUNSTABLE LLC

© TM ®

To: SD

Date: 9-10-YR-3 Time: 9:20 A

While You Were Out

M:s Point

Of:

Phone No.: 367-2787

Telephoned ☒ Please Call ☒

Called to See You ☐ Will Call Again ☐

Wants to See You ☐ Urgent ☐

Returned Your Call ☐

Message:

SD Returned Call ☐ Per: HM

Exhibit 13B

Telephone Message Slip, Dated September 14, YR-3

LAW OFFICES OF STANLEY DUNSTABLE LLC

© TM ®

To: SD

Date: 9-14-YR-3 Time: 10:50A

While You Were Out

M: Point

Of:

Phone No.: 367-2787

Telephoned	☒	Please Call	☒
Called to See You	☐	Will Call Again	☐
Wants to See You	☐	Urgent	☒
Returned Your Call	☐		

Message:

SD Returned Call ☐ Per: Hm

Exhibit 13C

Telephone Message Slip, Dated September 18, YR-3

LAW OFFICES OF STANLEY DUNSTABLE LLC

© ™ ®

To: SD

Date: 9-18-YR-3 Time: 8:50A

While You Were Out

MS Point

Of:

Phone No.:

Telephoned	☒	Please Call	☒
Called to See You	☐	Will Call Again	☐
Wants to See You	☐	Urgent	☒ X
Returned Your Call	☐		

Message:

SD Returned Call ☐ Per: Hm

Exhibit 13D

Telephone Message Slip, Dated September 25, YR-3

LAW OFFICES OF STANLEY DUNSTABLE LLC

© ™ ®

To: SD

Date: 9-25-YR-3 Time: 5:15 P

While You Were Out

M: Point

Of:

Phone No.:

Telephoned	☒	Please Call	☐
Called to See You	☐	Will Call Again	☐
Wants to See You	☐	Urgent	☒ X X
Returned Your Call	☐		

Message: She's getting pretty mad!

SD Returned Call ☐ Per: Hm

Exhibit 14A

Point Arbitration Exhibit A—Still Frame from ***The Red Balloon***

Due to printing limitations, Exhibits 14A, 14B, and 14C are reproduced in this book in black and white. Readers should understand that, per the facts of the case, the balloon is red in Exhibit 14A, white in Exhibit 14B, and pink in Exhibit 14C. Please refer to the downloadable exhibits, as they accurately reflect the colors in each exhibit.

Exhibit 14B

Point Arbitration Exhibit B—Still Frame from *What Red Balloon?*

Photo © Adrian Mendoza Photography, www.amenfoto.com.
Used by kind permission of the photographer.

Exhibit 14C

Point Arbitration Exhibit C—Still Frame from *What Red Balloon?*, as Colorized by MajorFilms

Photo © Adrian Mendoza Photography, www.amenfoto.com.
Used by kind permission of the photographer.

Exhibit 15

Contingent Fee Agreement

LAW OFFICES OF STANLEY DUNSTABLE LLC

© ™ ®

FOR LEGAL SERVICES RENDERED

To: Ms. Joséphine Point
91 Mansfield St
Nita City, NI 02220

March 5, YR-2

For Legal Services Rendered for the period March YR-4 through June YR-4:

Initial consultation re proposed Distributorship Agreement with MajorFilms, Inc; research provisions of Distributorship Agreement in *Gilliam v. ABC*; drafting of proposed clauses for insertion into Agreement; telephone consultations

S. Dunstable - 6 hours @ $400/hour	$ 2,400.00
Expenses: mail, LD telephone, copying	46.50
	$ 2,446.50

For Legal Services Rendered for the period February YR-3 through November YR-3:

Initial consultation re arbitration vs. MajorFilms, Inc.; drafting of Demand for Arbitration; paralegal research of proposed arbitrators; preparation of testimony of Ms. Point and expert witness Sullivan; review of Sullivan's report; paralegal preparation of exhibits; attorney review of exhibits; preparation of arbitration; attendance at arbitration

S. Dunstable – 36 hours @ $400/hour	$14,400.00
P. Porter – 3 hours @ $100/hour	300.00
Expenses: mail, LD telephone, copying	437.75
	$15,137.75
TOTAL:	**$17,584.25**

Terms: Payment due within 30 days; subject to interest of 1½% monthly thereafter.

Final Jury Instructions

1. Members of the jury, I shall now instruct you on the law that you must follow in reaching your verdict. It is your duty as jurors to decide the issues, and only those issues, that I submit for determination by your verdict. In reaching your verdict, you should consider and weigh the evidence, decide the disputed issues of fact, and apply the law on which I shall instruct you to the facts as you find them from the evidence.

2. The evidence in this case consists of the sworn testimony of the witnesses, all exhibits and other evidence received in evidence, and all the facts that may be admitted or agreed to by the parties. In determining the facts, you may draw reasonable inferences from the evidence. You may make deductions and reach conclusions that reason and common sense lead you to draw from the facts shown by the evidence in this case, but you may not speculate on any matters outside the evidence.

3. Joséphine Point, the plaintiff, has brought this professional negligence claim against Stanley Dunstable, the defendant. It is the plaintiff's claim that the defendant was careless, negligent, and failed to act with the ordinary skill and competence of an attorney engaged in the practice of law in the State of Nita in her representation of the plaintiff by:

    a. Failing to abide by Point's desire, which she claims was express, to make a primary goal of her arbitration against MajorFilms, Inc. ("the Arbitration") the advancement of the doctrine of *droit moral* as a legal theory for protecting artists' rights generally, and her rights specifically, from alteration, degradation, or mutilation of their artistic works;

    b. Failing to use the doctrine of *droit moral* as a ground for relief in the Arbitration, which failure the plaintiff claims was a substantial factor in causing her to lose the Arbitration;

    c. Failing to investigate adequately the background of the proposed arbitrators and of MajorFilms's expert witness and, as a consequence, failing to discover conflicts of interest and biases that the plaintiff claims affected the outcome of the Arbitration;

    d. Failing to communicate adequately and timely with the plaintiff concerning, inter alia, the arbitrators' backgrounds; the previous and likely continuing close affiliation of Arbitration Chairperson Primus and MajorFilms's expert witness; Dunstable's decision and reasons for not advancing the doctrine of *droit moral* in derogation of the plaintiff's claimed express goal for the Arbitration; the risk that the plaintiff would be required to pay the Arbitration fees and expenses, which in fact were imposed on her in the amount of twenty-seven thousand dollars ($27,000); and the true nature of his handling of a previous similar case; and

    e. Such other failures as the plaintiff has sought to prove at trial.

4. The plaintiff claims that as a result of the professional negligence of the defendant, she suffered the loss of the Arbitration, damage to her professional and artistic reputation, and such other damages as she sought to prove at trial.

5. The defendant denies all of the plaintiff's claims and asserts that at all times he acted with the ordinary skill and competence of a lawyer practicing in the State of Nita.

6. The plaintiff has the burden of proving that it is more likely true than not true that:
    a. An attorney-client relationship existed between the defendant and the plaintiff. In this case, it is undisputed that the attorney-client relationship existed.
    b. The defendant did not exercise the care and judgment of a reasonable attorney possessed of legal skill and knowledge in similar circumstances;
    c. The defendant's failure of the exercise of the required standard of care was a substantial factor in causing the harm to the plaintiff that the plaintiff has alleged and sought to prove.
7. Legal professional negligence consists of negligent or unskilled performance by an attorney of the duties undertaken by her on behalf of her client, or a lack of proper care and skill in the performance of a professional act of representation.
8. An attorney is obligated to exercise that degree of care, skill, and diligence that is exercised by prudent practicing attorneys in the jurisdiction in which she is licensed to practice law.
9. An attorney is not required to exercise perfect professional judgment in every instance. However, the attorney's license to practice law and her contract of employment hold out to the client that she possesses certain skills, knowledge, and abilities commensurate with those of similarly situated practicing attorneys in the State.
10. The duties imposed by law on an attorney are to possess and employ in the handling of the client's legal affairs such reasonable skill and knowledge usually possessed by attorneys in the same jurisdiction in which she is licensed to practice law. In employing the required skills and knowledge, she is also required to exercise the care and judgment of a reasonable attorney possessed of legal skill and knowledge in similar circumstances. This duty applies to all conduct in the representation of a client in a matter, including, but not limited to, case investigation, providing legal advice to the client, and all aspects of the litigation and trial of the matter.
11. While proof of a violation of a rule regulating the conduct of lawyers (e.g., the Nita Rules of Professional Conduct) does not give rise to an implied cause of action for legal malpractice—also known as "professional negligence"—it may nevertheless be considered by you as the trier of fact as an aid in understanding and applying the standard of negligence set forth in Instruction 10, to the extent that: a) the rule was designed for the protection of persons in the position of the plaintiff, and b) proof of the content and construction of such a rule is relevant to the plaintiff's claim.
12. The Nita Rules of Professional Conduct include the following provisions:

    (Counsel may rely on and argue any of the excerpts from NRPC included in Appendix A hereto.)
13. Defendant has counterclaimed against the Plaintiff, alleging that she has failed to pay his outstanding invoice for legal fees and expenses. In your deliberations, you should consider and decide whether the defendant has proved his counterclaim.
14. It is now your responsibility to deliberate and, if you agree, return a verdict in this case. Your verdict should concern liability only and must be unanimous.

IN THE SUPERIOR COURT

FOR THE COUNTY OF DARROW

NITA

JOSÉPHINE POINT, Plaintiff	:	CIVIL ACTION YR-2-1427
	:	
	:	
	:	
STANLEY DUNSTABLE, Defendant	:	JURY TRIAL DEMANDED

VERDICT—LIABILITY

On the Plaintiff's Claim:

We, the jury, unanimously find:

For the Plaintiff ________

For the Defendant ________

On the Defendant's Counterclaim:

We, the jury, unanimously find:

For the Plaintiff ________

For the Defendant ________

____

Foreperson

APPENDIX A

EXCERPTS FROM
NITA RULES OF PROFESSIONAL CONDUCT

Scope

. . . .

(20) Violation of a Rule should not itself give rise to a cause of action against a lawyer nor should it create any presumption in such a case that a legal duty has been breached. The Rules . . . are not designed to be a basis for civil liability. . . . Nevertheless, since the Rules do establish standards of conduct by lawyers, a lawyer's violation of a Rule may be evidence of breach of the applicable standard of conduct.

. . . .

RULE 1.0 Terminology

. . . .

(e) "Informed consent" denotes the agreement by a person to a proposed course of conduct after the lawyer has communicated adequate information and explanation about the material risks of and reasonably available alternatives to the proposed course of conduct.

(f) "Knowingly," "known," or "knows" denotes actual knowledge of the fact in question. A person's knowledge may be inferred from circumstances.

. . . .

(h) "Reasonable" or "reasonably" when used in relation to conduct by a lawyer denotes the conduct of a reasonably prudent and competent lawyer.

(i) "Reasonable belief" or "reasonably believes" when used in reference to a lawyer denotes that the lawyer believes the matter in question and that the circumstances are such that the belief is reasonable.

(j) "Reasonably should know" when used in reference to a lawyer denotes that a lawyer of reasonable prudence and competence would ascertain the matter in question.

. . . .

RULE 1.1 Competence

A lawyer shall provide competent representation to a client competent representation requires the legal knowledge, skill, thoroughness, and preparation reasonably necessary for the representation.

Comment

Legal Knowledge and Skill

(1) In determining whether a lawyer employs the requisite knowledge and skill in a particular matter, relevant factors include the relative complexity and specialized nature of the matter, the lawyer's general experience, the lawyer's training and experience in the field in question, the preparation and study the lawyer is able to give the matter and whether it is feasible to refer the matter to, or associate or consult with, a lawyer of established competence in the field in question. In many instances, the required proficiency is that of a general practitioner. Expertise in a particular field of law may be required in some circumstances.

(2) A lawyer need not necessarily have special training or prior experience to handle legal problems of a type with which the lawyer is unfamiliar. A newly admitted lawyer can be as competent as a practitioner with long experience. Some important legal skills, such as the analysis of precedent, the evaluation of evidence and legal drafting, are required in all legal problems. Perhaps the most fundamental legal skill consists of determining what kind of legal problems a situation may involve, a skill that necessarily transcends any particular specialized knowledge. A lawyer can provide adequate representation in a wholly novel field through necessary study. Competent representation can also be provided through the association of a lawyer of established competence in the field in question.

. . . .

(4) A lawyer may accept representation where the requisite level of competence can be achieved by reasonable preparation. . . .

Thoroughness and Preparation

(5) Competent handling of a particular matter includes inquiry into and analysis of the factual and legal elements of the problem, and use of methods and procedures meeting the standards of competent practitioners. It also includes adequate preparation. The required attention and preparation are determined in part by what is at stake; major litigation and complex transactions ordinarily require more extensive treatment than matters of lesser complexity and consequence. An agreement between the lawyer and the client regarding the scope of the representation may limit the matters for which the lawyer is responsible. *See* Rule 1.2(c).

Maintaining Competence

(6) To maintain the requisite knowledge and skill, a lawyer should keep abreast of changes in the law and its practice, engage in continuing study and education and comply with all continuing legal education requirements to which the lawyer is subject.

RULE 1.2 Scope of Representation and Allocation of Authority Between Client and Lawyer

(a) Subject to paragraph[ ] (c) . . . , a lawyer shall abide by a client's decisions concerning the objectives of representation and, as required by Rule 1.4, shall consult with the client as to the

means by which they are to be pursued. A lawyer may take such action on behalf of the client as is impliedly authorized to carry out the representation. . . .

. . . .

(c) A lawyer may limit the scope of the representation if the limitation is reasonable under the circumstances and the client gives informed consent.

. . . .

Comment

Allocation of Authority between Client and Lawyer

(1) Paragraph (a) confers upon the client the ultimate authority to determine the purposes to be served by legal representation, within the limits imposed by law and the lawyer's professional obligations. The decisions specified in paragraph (a), such as whether to settle a civil matter, must also be made by the client. See Rule 1.4(a)(1) for the lawyer's duty to communicate with the client about such decisions. With respect to the means by which the client's objectives are to be pursued, the lawyer shall consult with the client as required by Rule 1.4(a)(2) and may take such action as is impliedly authorized to carry out the representation.

(2) On occasion, however, a lawyer and a client may disagree about the means to be used to accomplish the client's objectives. Clients normally defer to the special knowledge and skill of their lawyer with respect to the means to be used to accomplish their objectives, particularly with respect to technical, legal and tactical matters. Conversely, lawyers usually defer to the client regarding such questions as the expense to be incurred and concern for third persons who might be adversely affected. Because of the varied nature of the matters about which a lawyer and client might disagree and because the actions in question may implicate the interests of a tribunal or other persons, this Rule does not prescribe how much disagreements are to be resolved. Other law, however, may be applicable and should be consulted by the lawyer. The lawyer should also consult with the client and seek a mutually acceptable resolution of the disagreement. If such efforts are unavailing and the lawyer has a fundamental disagreement with the client, the lawyer may withdraw from the representation. . . . Conversely, the client may resolve the disagreement by discharging the lawyer. . . .

. . . .

RULE 1.3 Diligence

A lawyer shall act with reasonable diligence and promptness in representing a client.

Comment

(1) A lawyer should pursue a matter on behalf of a client despite opposition, obstruction or personal inconvenience to the lawyer, and take whatever lawful and ethical measures are required to vindicate a client's cause or endeavor. A lawyer must also act with commitment and dedication to the interests of the client and with zeal in advocacy upon the client's behalf. A lawyer is not bound, however, to press for

every advantage that might be realized for a client. For example, a lawyer may have authority to exercise professional discretion in determining the means by which a matter should be pursued. See Rule 1.2. The lawyer's duty to act with reasonable diligence does not require the use of offensive tactics or preclude the treating of all persons involved in the legal process with courtesy and respect.

(2) A lawyer's work load must be controlled so that each matter can be handled competently.

(3) Perhaps no professional shortcoming is more widely resented than procrastination. A client's interests often can be adversely affected by the passage of time or the change of conditions; in extreme instances, as when a lawyer overlooks a statute of limitations, the client's legal position may be destroyed. Even when the client's interests are not affected in substance, however, unreasonable delay can cause a client needless anxiety and undermine confidence in the lawyer's trustworthiness. . . .

. . . .

RULE 1.4 Communication

(a) A lawyer shall:

(1) promptly inform the client of any decision or circumstance with respect to which the client's informed consent, as defined in Rule 1.0(e), is required by these Rules;

(2) reasonably consult with the client about the means by which the client's objectives are to be accomplished;

(3) keep the client reasonably informed about the status of the matter; [and]

(4) promptly comply with reasonable requests for information;. . . .

. . . .

(b) A lawyer shall explain a matter to the extent reasonably necessary to permit the client to make informed decisions regarding the representation.

Comment

(1) Reasonable communication between the lawyer and the client is necessary for the client effectively to participate in the representation.

Communicating with Client

(2) If these Rules require that a particular decision about the representation be made by the client, paragraph (a)(1) requires that the lawyer promptly consult with and secure the client's consent prior to taking action unless prior discussions with the client have resolved what action the client wants the lawyer to take. . . .

(3) Paragraph (a)(2) requires the lawyer to reasonably consult with the client about the means to be used to accomplish the client's objectives. In some situations—depending on both the importance of the action under consideration and the feasibility of consulting with the client—this duty will require consultation prior to taking action. In other circumstances, such as during a trial when an immediate decision must be made, the exigency of the situation may require the lawyer to act without prior consultation. In such cases, the lawyer must nonetheless act reasonably to inform the client of actions the lawyer has taken on the client's behalf. Additionally, paragraph (a)(3) requires that the lawyer keep the client reasonably informed about the status of the matter, such as significant developments affecting the timing or the substance of the representation.

(4) A lawyer's regular communication with clients will minimize the occasions on which a client will need to request information concerning the representation. When a client makes a reasonable request for information, however, paragraph (a)(4) requires prompt compliance with the request, or if a prompt response is not feasible, that the lawyer, or a member of the lawyer's staff, acknowledge receipt of the request and advise the client when a response may be expected. Client telephone calls should be promptly returned or acknowledged.

Explaining Matters

(5) The client should have sufficient information to participate intelligently in decisions concerning the objectives of the representation and the means by which they are to be pursued, to the extent the client is willing and able to do so. Adequacy of communication depends in part on the kind of advice or assistance that is involved. . . . In litigation a lawyer should explain the general strategy and prospects of success and ordinarily should consult the client on tactics that are likely to result in significant expense. . . . On the other hand, a lawyer ordinarily will not be expected to describe trial or negotiation strategy in detail. The guiding principle is that the lawyer should fulfill reasonable client expectations for information consistent with the duty to act in the client's best interests, and the client's overall requirements as to the character of representation. In certain circumstances, such as when a lawyer asks a client to consent to a representation affected by a conflict of interest, the client must give informed consent, as defined in Rule 1.0(e);

(6) Ordinarily, the information to be provided is that appropriate for a client who is a comprehending and responsible adult. . . . Where many routine matters are involved, a system of limited or occasional reporting may be arranged with the client.

Withholding Information

(7) In some circumstances, a lawyer may be justified in delaying transmission of information when the client would be likely to react imprudently to an immediate communication. . . . A lawyer may not withhold information to serve the lawyer's own interest or convenience or the interests or convenience of another person. . . .

RULE 1.7 Conflict of Interest: Current Clients

(a) Except as provided in paragraph (b), a lawyer shall not represent a client if the representation involves a concurrent conflict of interest. A concurrent conflict of interest exists if:

. . . .

(2) there is a significant risk that the representation of one or more clients will be materially limited by the lawyer's responsibilities to another client, a former client or a third person or by a personal interest of the lawyer.

(b) Notwithstanding the existence of a concurrent conflict of interest under paragraph (a), a lawyer may represent a client if:

(1) the lawyer reasonably believes that the lawyer will be able to provide competent and diligent representation to each affected client;

(2) the representation is not prohibited by law; [and]

. . . .

(4) each affected client gives informed consent, confirmed in writing.

Comment

. . . .

Personal Interest Conflicts

(10) The lawyer's own interests should not be permitted to have an adverse effect on representation of a client. For example, if the probity of a lawyer's own conduct in a transaction is in serious question, it may be difficult or impossible for the lawyer to give a client detached advice. . . .

Appendix B

Legal Addendum

A. *Gilliam v. American Broadcasting Companies, Inc.*, 892 F.2d 202 (2d Cir. YR-21) (excerpt)

Plaintiffs, the writers and performers of the Monty Python television skit series that is a popular feature of British television (hereafter, "the Pythons"), brought this action to enjoin ABC-TV's broadcasting of selected Monty Python skits, on the ground that ABC had edited and abridged the skits in a way that fundamentally altered the artists' intent and work. The trial court held that the Pythons had failed to establish the likelihood of success on the merits of their claim and denied the injunction. We reverse.

The agreement under which the Pythons granted ABC the right to air the Python skits on American television contained certain provisions governing what alterations could be made to the skits in order to adapt them to the differing format of U.S. television, especially the need to make time for commercials (which, on the UK BBC television channels, do not exist). We need not parse the agreement closely for purposes of our present review, because our review convinces us that the Pythons' evidence shows a clear violation of their artistic rights that cannot be harmonized with the agreement's provisions, and that the Pythons are entitled to the relief they seek.

* * *

Among other grounds for relief, it seems likely that the Pythons will succeed on the theory that, regardless of the right ABC had to alter and edit the programs, the cuts that ABC made constituted an actionable mutilation of the Pythons' work. This cause of action, which seeks redress for deformation of an artist's work, finds its roots in the continental concept of droit moral, which may generally be summarized as including the right of the artist to have his work attributed to him in the form in which he created it.

American copyright law, as presently written, does not recognize moral rights or provide a cause of action for their violation, since that body of law seeks to vindicate the economic, rather than the personal, rights of artists. Nevertheless, the economic incentive for artistic and intellectual creation that serves as the foundation for American copyright law cannot be reconciled with the inability of artists to obtain relief for mutilation or misrepresentation of their work to the public on which the artists are financially dependent. Thus courts have long granted relief for misrepresentation of an artist's work by relying on theories outside the statutory law of copyright, such as contract law, *Granz v. Harris*, 198 F.2d 585 (2d Cir. YR-58) (substantial cutting of original work constitutes misrepresentation), or the tort of unfair competition, *Prouty v. National Broadcasting Co.*, 26 F. Supp. 265 (D. Mass. YR-71). Although such decisions are clothed in terms of proprietary right in one's creation, they also properly vindicate the author's personal right to prevent the presentation of his work to the public in a distorted form. See *Gardella v. Log Cabin Products Co.*, 89 F.2d 891 (2d Cir. YR-73); Roeder, *The Doctrine of Moral Right*, 53 Harv. L. Rev. 554 (YR-70).

The law of these cases and authorities supports the granting of relief where a television network broadcasts a program properly designated as having been written and performed by a group, but which has been edited, without the artists' consent, into a form that departs substantially from the original work. "To deform his work is to present him to the public as the creator of a work not his own, and thus makes him subject to criticism for work he has not done." Roeder, *supra*, at 569. In such a case, it is the writer or performer, rather than the network, who suffers the consequences of the mutilation, for the public will have only the final product by which to evaluate the work.

During the hearing on the preliminary injunction, the trial court received as evidence the edited version of the Monty Python program broadcast by ABC and the original, unedited version. We find that the truncated version at times omitted the climax of the skits to which the Pythons' rare brand of humor was leading and at other times deleted essential elements in the schematic development of a story line.[9] We therefore hold that the edited version broadcast by ABC impaired the integrity of the Pythons' work and represented to the public as the Pythons' product what was actually a mere caricature of their talents. We believe that a valid cause of action for such distortion exists and that therefore a preliminary injunction may issue to prevent repetition of the broadcast prior to final determination of the issues.

B. *Turner Entertainment Co. v. Huston, CA Versailles [France]*, civ. ch., December 19, YR-16 (translated excerpt)

The cinematographic work entitled *Asphalt Jungle* was produced in YR-60 [1950] in the U.S. by the MGM Company. The film was shot in black and white by the late John Huston, a movie director of American nationality, at the time bound by contract to MGM. MGM obtained from the U.S. Copyright Office a certificate of registration of its rights to the film. In YR-24, the benefit of this registration was transferred to Turner Entertainment Co. by virtue of its merger with MGM.

Turner had the movie colorized and announced that it would broadcast this colorized version on the French television station Fifth French Television Channel (La Cinq SA) in June YR-22. The broadcast was objected to by Mr. Huston's heirs, Anjelica, Daniel, and Walter Huston, who opposed the broadcast because they deemed it a violation of the author's moral right, aggravated in their opinion by the fact that John Huston had opposed colorization of this works during his life.

The judges in first instance in the present case have precisely pointed out that the aesthetic conception which earned John Huston his great fame is based on the interplay of black and white, which enabled him to create an atmosphere according to which he directed the actor and selected the backdrops; moreover, he expressed himself clearly about his film entitled The Maltese

9. A single example will illustrate the extent of distortion engendered by the editing. In one skit, an upper-class English family is engaged in a discussion of the tonal quality of certain words as "woody" or "tinny." The father soon begins to suggest certain words with sexual connotations as either "woody" or "tinny," whereupon the mother fetches a bucket of water and pours it over his head. The skit continues from this point. The ABC edit eliminates the middle sequence—apparently to avoid the use of the sexual innuendoes—so that the father is comfortably dressed at one moment and, in the next moment, is shown in a soaked condition without any explanation for the change in his appearance.

Falcon when stating, "I wanted to shoot it in black and white like a sculptor chooses to work in clay, to pour his work in bronze, to sculpt in marble."

In YR-60 [1950], while color film technique was already widespread and another option was available, the film entitled *Asphalt Jungle* was shot in black and white, following a deliberate aesthetic choice, according to a process which its author considered best suited to the character of the work.

Therefore, the film's colorization without authorization and control by the author or his heirs amounted to violation of the creative activity of its maker, even if it should satisfy the expectations of a certain public for commercially obvious reasons; the use of this process without the agreement of Messrs and Mrs Huston infringed the moral right of the author as mandatorily protected under French law; Messrs and Mrs Huston have therefore good grounds to petition the court for reparation of their prejudice at the hands of the Turner Company, and they will therefore be allotted FRF 400,000 [= 61,000 = $87,700] by way of damages and costs for the damage done; moreover, the judges recognize their right to demand that La Cinq SA be forbidden to broadcast the modified version of the film entitled *Asphalt Jungle*.

C. *Alison v. Jerome*, 450 Nita 38 (YR-6) (excerpt)

To prove a legal malpractice case, a plaintiff must prove by a preponderance of the evidence that the defendant's failure to exercise that degree of care, skill, and diligence that is exercised by prudent practicing attorneys in the jurisdiction in which he is licensed to practice law was a substantial factor in causing the harm to the plaintiff that plaintiff alleges and seeks to prove.

D. *Milstein v. Kay & Young, P.C.*, 339 Nita 444 (YR-11) (excerpt)

A violation of the NRPC is not negligence per se in a legal malpractice case. However, the NRPC, and any violation thereof, are relevant evidence in determining whether a lawyer has committed legal malpractice and may be considered by the trier of fact as an aid in understanding and applying the standard of negligence, to the extent that: (a) the rule was designed for the protection of persons in the position of the plaintiff, and (b) proof of the content and construction of such a rule is relevant to the plaintiff's claim.

E. *Hildebrand Enterprises Co. v. Gama Gama Gama, Inc.*, 316 Nita 35 (YR-17) (excerpt)

Nita's statutory form of the parol evidence rule, 64 Ni. T.S. § 1946, makes inadmissible oral or written extrinsic evidence of prior or contemporaneous agreements offered to alter or modify a written instrument, such as a contract, if that instrument has become integrated by the parties having manifested their intent to supersede all prior or contemporaneous agreements and to constitute the written instrument as the final, complete, and exclusive embodiment of their agreement. However, where a term of the integrated agreement is ambiguous, admitting of more than one interpretation or meaning, the parol evidence rule does not bar the use of oral or written extrinsic evidence to explain or clarify such term.

F. *Restatement of the Law (3d) Governing Lawyers*, § 21

Allocating the Authority to Decide Between a Client and a Lawyer

As between client and lawyer:

(1) A client and lawyer may agree which of them will make specified decisions. . . . This agreement may be superseded by another valid agreement.

(2) A client may instruct a lawyer during the representation . . . .

(3) Subject to Subsections (1) and (2) a lawyer may take any lawful measure within the scope of representation that is reasonably calculated to advance a client's objectives as defined by the client, consulting with the client as required . . . .

. . . .

Comment

. . . .

b. *Rationale.* Allocation of authority between client and lawyer can influence both the outcome of a representation and the balances of power and respect within it. What allocation of authority a client desires may vary from client to client, from lawyer to lawyer, from case to case, and from issue to issue.

The lawyer begins with broad authority to make choices advancing the client's interests. But the client may limit the lawyer's authority by contract or instructions . . . .

. . . .

d. *Client instructions.* A client may give instructions to a lawyer during the representation about matters within the lawyer's reasonable power to perform . . . . As the client learns about the lawyer during the representation, the client may modify instructions to the lawyer accordingly.

. . . A lawyer may advise a client of the advantages and disadvantages of a proposed client decision and seek to dissuade the client from adhering to it . . . . However, a lawyer may not continue a representation while refusing to follow a client's continuing instruction . . . . A lawyer may, after obtaining the required court permission, withdraw from the representation if the instructions are considered repugnant or imprudent . . . or render the representation unreasonably difficult . . . .

www.ingramcontent.com/pod-product-compliance
Lightning Source LLC
Chambersburg PA
CBHW081126180926
51611CB00004B/64